The Duino Elegies

RAINER MARIA RILKE

The Duino Elegies

TRANSLATED BY
STEPHEN GARMEY AND JAY WILSON
WITH AN INTRODUCTION AND COMMENTARY
DRAWN FROM RILKE'S LETTERS
ARRANGED AND TRANSLATED BY
STEPHEN GARMEY

HARPER COLOPHON BOOKS
HARPER & ROW, PUBLISHERS
NEW YORK, EVANSTON, SAN FRANCISCO, LONDON

Acknowledgments

The translators would like to thank Marianne Moore, Eugen Kullmann, and Adolf K. Placzek for their help in bringing the original more precisely into English.

FIRST EDITION: HARPER COLOPHON BOOKS, 1972

LIBRARY OF CONGRESS CATALOG CARD NUMBER: 76-168938

STANDARD BOOK NUMBER: 06-090254-X

The German text does not accompany these translations only because every effort to obtain permission to print it failed. The reader is urged to seek out a copy of the original poems so that he may at least hear the sound of the true *Duino Elegies*.

CONTENTS

The Duino Elegies

INTRODUCTION

Rilke wrote the first of his *Duino Elegies* in January 1912 at the castle of his friend, Princess Marie von Thurn und Taxis-Hohenlohe at Duino near Trieste, which was then still part of Austria. The preceding September Princess Marie had written offering him the use of Duino, and from Munich he had replied:

Your letter, Princess, which put Duino before me like a great solitary prospect, was exactly what I needed. In Berlin things did not go as I had wanted, and here I am all tied up in a bundle of anxieties, right in the middle like one of them, and I can't move. . . . The necessity to be alone, alone for a long time, builds stronger in me every day. Not to speak, not to look up, save into the faceless, into the outspread ocean, the sea—that will be the right thing for me. People (whether it be my fault or theirs) wear me out; in Leipzig, as here, there was always someone who couldn't cope with certain things and would drop them right in my lap. And it's no good to push these things away, for then people want to know what I do about them myself—as though I were so correct I should erect a monument and write an inscription for it as well. I am exhausted with it all. What a blessing you are willing to hide me away in Duino: I will hole up there like a fugitive, go by a strange name, and only you will know it is I.[1]

Princess Marie lent Rilke her car and chauffeur to drive down from Paris to Duino. She wrote in her memoirs that he was driven at a snail's pace through Provence, and that she was waiting at Duino to welcome him. The second week in December she left for Vienna, and Rilke stayed on alone. He wrote to her on December 15:

I spend much of my time in the park, and am nearly always out of doors. . . . Carlo looks after me; I eat in the hall near my room —he allows me this with the unending kindness of a big old dog who lets a little one eat out of his bowl. The cook was horrified the first day at my vegetarian pretensions, but we have both given way a little, and now she is getting over it and back to her art— today she was perfectly inventive. . . . Housekeeping goes on one place or another the whole day long, but not near me—here there is silence, a magic skein of silence. I had the flowers from your boudoir brought here and the ones that are left I keep beside me. . . . At seven I eat the most childlike supper; a little after nine and I am already in bed, God preserve my simplicity.[2]

Princess Marie writes that Carlo, the old servant, was very frightened when he heard Rilke walking up and down his room alone for hours,

reading out loud and scanning his verses, gesticulating violently. He didn't understand what was going on. . . . He believed he saw something of the devil in these monologues, to him so incomprehensible.[3]

Rilke wrote to a friend on December 14:

I shall have to try right here to clamber over the crest of the new year in the dark and all alone, for what you might call reasons of

1. *RMR-MTT*, i, 63–64 (dated September 17, 1911).
2. *Ibid.*, 75–76.
3. *Erinnerungen*, 40.

discipline. I have wanted for a long time to be here alone, strictly alone, to go into a chrysalis, to pull myself together; in a word, to live by the heart and nothing else. I have really been all alone since the day before yesterday inside these old walls—outside, the sea . . . the rain, perhaps tomorrow a storm: I should find out now what is in me to counterbalance such great and fundamental things. So if something quite unexpected does not come, won't it be the right thing to stay on, to hold out, to hold still with a kind of curiosity toward myself? That is how things stand, and if I were to move now, everything would shift again. And, of course, it is written on the heart, like on certain medicines, shake well before taking: I have been continually shaken these last few years, but never taken; therefore it is better for me to come in this stillness to clarity and precipitation.[4]

On December 30, he wrote to Princess Marie:

I see now for the first time where I have come in the two years I have not worked. . . . Solitude is a true elixir, it is now driving the disease right up to the surface; things must first become bad, then worse, then worst—no language carries it any further but then all will be well. I creep around all day in the thickets of my life, shouting like mad and clapping my hands—: you would not believe what hair-raising creatures fly up. . . . Fortunately we are having clear weather; I howl at the moon with all my heart and put the blame on the dogs. . . . I have a great desire to read these days; a little Shakespeare, whom I scarcely know yet—though he is too mountainous for me, too steep, too amorphous: I clamber and slip, and never know what exactly happens to me. Now I am turning the pages of Balzac's *Lettres à l'Etrangère* (in a German translation).[5]

Solitude was the indisputable climate for Rilke's creative powers. But until they became active, it meant a loneliness almost too difficult to bear. That very difficulty he tried to welcome, and adhere to its pain. It was the price of his art.

4. *B. 1907–1914*, 141–142.
5. *RMR-MTT*, i, 84–85.

On January 6 he wrote:

Today at half-past six, I am going to plunge again into the tunnel of solitude and see if I can find my footing. It is not so much that I am making the noise in the thickets, as that the noise is there while I live, breathe, pull myself together; it grinds and creaks like a mill running empty, and the nightingales . . . ? You know, Princess, they build for their lovers in the thorns, and thorns are not lacking here. The true nightingale builds its nest knowing that despite everything, there must be the still, stillest hours; it takes advantage of them. As soon as I hear one slightest attempt, I will stop all this old machinery, and be as gentle and great as the night itself. But that's just the problem. . . .[6]

Then on January 12 he continued:

now the divinely ordained solitude is really under way. Every day I become a little sharper: if someone were to come in now it would not be safe for him; perhaps I shall start biting next.[7]

And two days later:

this castle is an immense body without much soul; obsessed with the idea of its own firmness, it holds one with the inward-directed force of its own gravity like a prisoner. An evergreen garden climbs up to it along the steep cliffs; otherwise there is not much green . . . these hardened mountains renounce the effeminacy of vegetation . . . I long for work; sometimes I believe for a moment that it is longing for me—but we do not meet.[8]

Then came the breakthrough. Princess Marie later described it in her memoirs:

Rilke had not forseen what was preparing itself in him. A great sadness invaded him; he began to believe that this winter would come to nothing.

Then one morning, he received an annoying business letter. He

6. *Ibid.*, 88–89.
7. *Ibid.*, 90.
8. *B. 1907–1914*, 168.

wanted to dispose of it quickly, and so he had to deal with figures and other dull things. Outside a strong *bora* was blowing but the sun was shining and the sea was brilliant blue and spun with silver. He climbed down to the bastions jutting out over the sea to the east and west, which are connected by a narrow path to the foot of the castle. The rocks there fall off in a sheer drop, easily two hundred feet, down to the sea. He walked up and down entirely lost in thought, concerned with how he should answer the letter. Then all at once, in the midst of his brooding he suddenly stopped short, for it seemed to him that he had heard a voice calling to him out of the roaring of the wind: *Wer, wenn ich schriee, hörte mich denn aus der Engel Ordnungen?* . . . he took out the notebook he always carried with him and wrote down these words together with several more verses that formed themselves without any effort on his part. . . . He went back very quietly to his room, laid his notebook aside and dealt with the business letter. But by evening the entire elegy had been written down.[9]

He copied the First Elegy, as soon as it was written, into a small book with Louis XVI tooling that he and the Princess had bought together in Weimar, and sent it to her on January 21, with a note saying:

Now, dear Princess, the little green book comes back to you at last, to remain with you always, most arbitrarily filled with the first Duino work (and the first after so long!), for which it was precisely made. Accept it, be good to it, as you were from the first moment, although strictly speaking, it purported to be only the "Compendium of the General Precepts of Religion, 1801," which it contained. But we both saw that it had a higher, secret purpose.[10]

The Second Elegy came soon after the First, at the end of January or the beginning of February 1912. In it Rilke brings

9. Furstin Marie von Thurn und Taxis-Hohenlohe, *Erinnerungen an Rainer Maria Rilke* (München, 1937), pp. 40–41.
10. *RMR-MTT*, i, 97–98.

into sharp focus the difficulty and pain he experienced in any intimate relationship with another person.

He wrote to Lou Andreas-Salomé:

from a purely physical point of view I am just unbearable to myself; certain bad habits which I always used to reach through like bad air, are taking shape in my mind more and more, and I am afraid one day they will surround me like walls.[11]

Almost ten years before, Rilke and his wife had found the demands of art incompatible with those of their life together. She was now undergoing analysis in Vienna and her doctor, Baron von Gebsattel, had suggested that Rilke too might benefit from the experience. But with his wife it was

a different thing: her work has never helped her, whereas mine, in a certain sense, has been from the start a kind of self-treatment; though to be sure, the more elaborate and established it becomes, the more it loses its therapeutic and considerate nature and makes demands on me. A soul that is dependent for its harmony on the huge exaggerations of art, has to be able to rely on a body that does not ape it in any way, but is precise and simply does not exaggerate itself.[12]

I know that analysis would make sense for me only if I really took seriously that strange mental reservation *not to write any more,* which when I was finishing *Malte* I often dangled in front of my nose like a kind of relief. I could then exorcise my devils which at the level of ordinary everyday life are only irksome and painful. But the angels would probably go with them, and this I would have to take as another simplification and tell myself that in my next, new profession (which?) they would be of no use.[13]

He had written to von Gebsattel that, whatever the cost to himself, he couldn't risk frightening off his angels:

11. *RMR-LAS,* 260 (dated January 20, 1912).
12. *Ibid.,* 261.
13. *Ibid.,* 262–263 (dated January 24, 1912).

believe me, nothing grips me so much as the incomprehensible, un-heard-of wonder of my being alive at all, since from the beginning my life has been so impossibly laid out, proceeding from rescue to rescue, always, as it were, through the hardest stone. When I think of choosing not to write any more, the only thing that really dismays me is that I would no longer be recording the utterly wonderful line along which I've come through this strange life of mine. Around me I see bleak fates and hear talk of accidents, and can't escape wondering what it all means. Can you understand, my friend, how I am afraid to make any classification or survey that might make life easier, for fear of disturbing a much higher order whose right I've got to acknowledge, after all that has hap-pened, even if it should destroy me.[14]

Couldn't it be that given my disposition, there is only one entirely right thing to do: to hold out? I think I will be time after time in the position of Sinbad the Sailor who, in the doom of his predica-ments, swore off all travel and yet ever and again made ready one day and set out, he knew not how![15]

Before he left Duino that March Rilke had also produced fragments of what would later become the Third, Sixth, Ninth, and Tenth Elegies.

In October 1912 Rilke went to Spain and stayed first in Toledo, which made a profound impression on him, shaping the unconscious raw material of the emerging poems.

I will never be able to say what it is like here . . . (it would re-quire language which only the angels speak when they manage to get through to me). . . . [Toledo] is so far out in space . . . I have imprinted it all on myself as if tomorrow I had to know it forever, the bridges . . . this river and, transferred over across it, the exposed mass of landscape looking like something still being created. . . . You can imagine yourself meeting a lion on one of

14. *B. 1907–1914,* 170 (dated January 14, 1912).
15. *Ibid.,* 184 (dated January 24, 1912).

the lanes you have uncovered and finding him obligated to you because of something quite involuntary in your bearing.[16]

This incomparable city takes the trouble to hold within its walls the whole arid, undiminished, unconquered landscape, even this sheer mountain, this mountain of vision.—The earth emerges enormous and immediately outside the gate becomes world, creation, mountain, and gorge, Genesis. Over and over again this place makes me think of some prophet who gets up from dinner, from hospitality, from being together with people and immediately, on the very threshold of his house, prophesying comes over him, the immense seeing of ruthless visions—: that is the way nature behaves all around this city, yes, even here and there inside it, nature looks up and doesn't recognize the city and has visions.[17]

Rilke's private world, however, was

not sufficient to nourish and sustain anyone. Against precisely this, one must take up counterweights in order to be in the whole. Perhaps, sometime, out of the fragments one little by little brings to oneself, something like a world will be discovered in the overall perspective—but that is still a good way off. Now I am more than ever one-sided; lament has prevailed over me many times, and I know I can use its full strings only to play the whole jubilation which swells up behind everything that is difficult or painful or endured, without which the voices are not complete.[18]

Three years later in Munich, Rilke remembered

the Spanish landscape (the last I have fully experienced), Toledo . . . the external thing itself: tower, mountain, bridge already possessed of the unheard-of, matchless intensity of the inner equivalents by which one might have been able to depict it. Everywhere, appearance and vision almost coincided in the object; in each object a whole inner world came to light, as though an angel enclasping space were blind and gazing into himself. This world,

16. *RMR-MTT*, i, 218–219 (dated November 2, 1912).
17. *Ibid.*, 227 (dated November 13, 1912).
18. *B. 1907–1914*, 253–254 (dated November 17, 1912).

seen no more with human eyes but in the angel, is perhaps my real task.[19]

After a month in Toledo, Rilke went to Seville and Cordova and then Ronda, but the trip had already begun to tax him. He wrote to Princess Marie:

had I happened to have a "home" I would certainly have gone home, for every journey, especially one through Spain, requires a certain equilibrium, an assurance that you can rely on yourself. But my world completely collapses every moment, inside me, in my blood, and when I am in a strange place the strangeness is beyond all measure. . . . I must track down the cause of this *malaise,* and discover the source of this evil that is always following me. Because scarcely have I planted a little flower bed somewhere, than this turbulence rises again, floods it and leaves it desolate. And I know that a doctor could do what I can't do for myself, if he were the right doctor. Everything in me is so much of a piece that I can't be suffering in one area of myself and at the same time accomplish anything in another area. Basically I'm not at all enamored of suffering: pain deprives me of the world, so I am certainly not cut out to be a saint and haven't the least hope of spreading any odor of sanctity. . . .

the unique appearance of this town piled up on two sheer masses of rock divided by the tight, narrow river gorge . . . which not a single window dares to look into . . . surrounded by a wide valley busy with its faceted fields, evergreen oaks and olive-trees and, resting way beyond, the pure mountain range. . . . Today when I looked at those mountains, those slopes rising up in the clearest air, as though they were going to sing out, I had to remind myself what joy this would have propelled in me three years ago. . . . Now it is as if my heart has moved miles away— I see many things set out in its direction but I never hear whether they arrive or not. . . . It is my fate, so to speak, to pass by human things and arrive at the outside limit of experience at the edge

19. *B. 1914–1921,* 80 (dated October 27, 1915).

of the world. When I was in Cordova an ugly little dog in the last stages of pregnancy came up to me; she had nothing much to commend her and no doubt she was full of some accidental litter that no one would take any interest in; but she came up to me, difficult as it was for her, when we were alone together, and raised her eyes to beg me to look after her. They were enlarged from trouble and inwardness, and in them was really everything that goes beyond the individual, I don't know where—into the future or the incomprehensible. Things relaxed a little when I gave her the piece of sugar that went with my coffee, and incidentally, oh so incidentally, we said a kind of mass together. The act was nothing but giving and accepting, but the meaning and the seriousness and our communion with each other was unlimited. That kind of thing can happen only on earth, and it is good to have willingly been through it here, however uncertainly, however guiltily, however lacking anything heroic. In the end we will be wonderfully prepared for divine relationships.[20]

And yet,

I spoil everything—it seems to me sometimes, that I must be bringing too much violence to bear on my impressions. . . . I stay too long before them, I press them into my face, and yet they already are by nature impressions, aren't they, even if one only lets them lie quiet a while, *au lieu de me pénétrer les impressions me percent.*[21]

On January 7, 1913, Rilke wrote to his publisher:

The emergence of the elegies last year has drawn me, at least a little, into the confidence of whatever may be shaping itself in me, unutterably slowly, under the pretext of such great .devastation. . . . As far as the present trip goes, it naturally has difficulty spreading itself over such disarranged and uneven inner conditions. Nevertheless, I haven't a moment's doubt that I must do these changes the most urgent service. That will bring certain regions that have lain there for ages within reach of whatever is beginning

20. *RMR-MTT*, i, 244–246, 248–249 (dated December 17, 1912).
21. *RMR-LAS*, 284–285 (dated December 19, 1912).

to stir in me. . . . My most hopeful insight is, more or less, that
. . . a process of digging up the soil of my nature whereby the top-
most parts get to the very bottom [. . . is going on] though it
can express itself only as pain and exposure.[22]

Sometime that January, or at the beginning of February,
something of what was emerging in him got to the surface,
and he wrote the first thirty-one lines of what was to become,
nine years later, the Sixth Elegy. Then later that year in Paris
he wrote three lines which became the end of the poem.

The problems plaguing Rilke at Duino were still very
much with him when he got to Paris in February. They form
the background of the Third Elegy passages where he writes
about the violent passions that infest the dreams and the blood-
stream of a young boy, how his mother can comfort him when
he is still young. He had once written that every meeting with
his own mother was a kind of setback:

Whenever I have to see this lost, unreal woman so cut loose from
everything, who can't even grow old, I remember how even as a
child I struggled to get away from her, and dread deep inside my-
self that even after years and years of running and walking I am
still not far enough away from her. Somewhere inside me I still
have moments which are the other half of her atrophied gestures,
of those broken bits of memories she carries around within her. I
shudder at her absent-minded piety, her obstinate faith, at all those
caricatures and distortions she has clung to, herself as empty as a
dress, like a phantom, terrible. That I am still her child, that in
this washed-out wall belonging to nothing, some scarcely recogniz-
able wallpaper door was my entrance into the world—(if such an
entrance can actually lead into the world . . .)![23]

J. R. von Salis recalls that Rilke once confessed to Princess
Marie: "I am not a lover, perhaps because I didn't love my

22. *B. Verleger*, i, 193–194.
23. *RMR-LAS*, 143 (dated April 15, 1904).

mother."[24] He comments that "the Third Elegy grew out of reaction to his own mother experience, or in flight from it."[25]

The imagery of the Elegy may also have been influenced by experiences Rilke had had at Duino in the spring of 1912:

> We are in a realm of mist which has just fumed up like magic on a stage, right in the strongest midday sun, and since then all distances have gone, boats blow their foghorns some place out there, invisible, and dread each other. Only the smaller skiffs near the shore catch the diffuse light on their sails, holding on like apparitions awhile in the vague gray world. From time to time a soft filigree rain tries itself out; meanwhile, during the stillness the garden gingerly turns green, the yellow double jonquils push their way up inquisitively, stalks bent with haste, and in all but the evergreens the fine clear work prepared in the rising sap, comes to light.[26]

One day that spring, Rilke had gone over onto

> the densely wooded slope that reached down to the sea to the right of the castle, to an inlet bounded by the bizarre rock formation of the old ruins. Evergreen oaks, cypresses, laurel, olive, and fig trees grew rampant here, unrestrained and all tangled together. Strange flowers sometimes bloomed in the shadow of the trees. . . . He wandered absent-minded, dreaming, through the undergrowth and maze of briars, and suddenly found himself next to a huge old olive tree which he had never noticed before. . . . The next thing he knew he was leaning back into the tree, standing on its gnarled roots, his head propped against the branches. . . . An odd sensation came over him so that he was fixed to the spot, breathless, his heart pounding. It was as though he were extended into another life, a long time before, and that everything that had ever been lived or loved or suffered here was coming to him, surrounding him, storming him, demanding to live again in him. . . . "Time" ceased to exist; there was no distinction between what

24. *Rainer Maria Rilke, The Years in Switzerland,* p. 133.
25. *Ibid.,* p. 134.
26. *RMR-MTT,* i, 119–120 (dated March 2, 1912).

once was and now had come back, and the dark, formless present. The entire atmosphere seemed animated, seemed unearthly to him, thrusting in on him incessantly. And yet this unknown life was close to him somehow; he had to take part in it. . . .[27]

This was Princess Marie's account of what Rilke had told her about the experience. His own somewhat longer version was written on February 1, 1913.[28] On October 21 he wrote to Lou Andreas-Salomé:

somehow I am still the same person . . . none of my old possibilities are really wasted or lost, but perhaps actually all still there, only I don't for a while know how to use them. . . . I seem to myself rather like a photographic plate that has been exposed too long, because I am still wide open to this place, to this violent current flowing into me. . . . In fright I went straight off to Rouen on Sunday. I need a whole cathedral to drown me out. France in the provinces always has something reassuring for me, so many old houses in which I can play with the idea that I am at home as I go past, but then when I look at them they turn out to be mostly for rent. . . . I am afraid I can stay in Paris only by pretending I have come here for a few days without any responsibilities, to take it easy, take life as it comes. . . . I would be contented with everything were it all only mine again, did it not drain right out of me into yearning. It frightens me to think how much I've been living away from myself, as if I were always standing at a telescope attributing to everyone who comes along a bliss certainly not to be found in any of them: my bliss all along, the bliss I once had in my loneliest hours . . . I must begin all over again. Even in a schoolbook it helped to turn a new page; this one, Paris, is now so full of the most embarrassing mistakes, red on top of red. . . .[29]

On December 16, 1913 he wrote to Princess Marie how much he was looking forward to the return that next week of

27. Princess Marie von Thurn und Taxis-Hohenlohe, *Erinnerungen*, 45–46.
28. *Erlebnis* I, *G.W*. iv, 280 ff.
29. *RMR-LAS*, 315–316.

the *Mona Lisa* which had been stolen from the Louvre the previous year, saying that she was the only woman in Paris he could associate with.[30] He was trying to create around himself again the solitude within which he could work. Princess Marie wrote to invite him for Christmas; he did not go, and even wrote to her on December 27 begging her not to come to Paris, saying that he had taken a vow not to see anyone, not to open his mouth, except inwardly:

I am in the cocoon . . . as if my room were drifting with gossamer, everything I spin day and night enveloping me so that already I've become unrecognizable. Wait, please, please, for the next butterfly. You saw last fall in Berlin how sad and loathsome the caterpillar was, an abomination. If no butterfly comes out in the end,—well and good; I'll stay put in this miserly place and dream quietly to myself of the grand mourning cloak I had once thought I might become. If I don't fly out, someone else will: the good Lord wants only that there be flying; just who provides it is of only passing interest to him. . . . I see no one. Outside it is icy, then it rains and drips—that is what winter is like here, always three days of each. I have had more than my fill of Paris, it's a place of damnation; I have always known that. Before, the pains of the damned were explained to me by an angel, but now when I am supposed to come to terms with them myself, I find no very creditable interpretation and in addition I am in danger of making the conception that was once so great, rather *minesquin*. If God has any consideration for me he should let me find a few rooms in the country where I can rave the way I like, and where the Elegies can howl out of me at the moon from all sides, just as they please.[31]

There is no record of just when the Third Elegy came into precise focus, out of the blur of these various images and experiences; to the best of our knowledge, Rilke never let any of his friends know.

30. *RMR-MTT*, i, 336.
31. *Ibid.*, 344–345.

On December 29 he wrote to Anton Kippenberg, his publisher:

My situation is this. . . . I can't predict anything, I get up day after day and try myself out in the quietest, most regular things, see no one, expect nothing of myself. But I know, in fact I have a definite sense of which palaces must be illuminated and royally inhabited, if the least gleam of light is to get out into the unbelieving world and fall on some small corner for a future poem.[32]

And the next day he wrote:

my days go by one after another with a few slow things to show for them, some pages translated from French, Italian, Danish, some indispensable letters. . . .[33]

The Third Elegy was apparently not finished. Yet in Rilke's notes it is dated "Paris, 1913." In the same letter of December 30 is a line that comes very close to the imagery of the poem:

I have a longing to turn right around and come back to myself: would I not find here an abandoned heart fallen into ruins in the midst of that vast forest which was childhood. . . .[34]

It may well be that as the year turned he was able to pull together the existing fragments and complete the Elegy.

The Fourth Elegy was written on November 22 and 23, 1915, in Munich where Rilke had moved at the outbreak of World War I. To begin with he had been dazed by the catastrophe and even written poems in praise of the "wargod," influenced by Hölderlin whom he had been reading.

In the first days of August [1914] the spectacle of the war, of the war-god, seized me `. . . now it is . . . no more a god, but the unleashing of a god over the people. Nothing more can be ac-

32. B. Verleger, i, 247–248.
33. B. 1907–1914, 323.
34. Ibid., 322.

complished now than for the soul to survive. Affliction and disaster
are perhaps no more present now than before, only more tangible,
more active, more apparent. For the affliction in which mankind
has daily lived from the very beginning, can't really be increased
no matter what the circumstances. Insight into man's unspeakable
misery does increase however, and perhaps this is what everything
is leading to today; so great a downfall—as though new risings
were seeking clearance and room for launching![35]

It was not art, however, that was to come forward with
that increase of insight. Rilke, like most European artists,
was unable to create anything that could even begin to trans-
form the world, or have any effect on the barbarism unleashed
in those days. He was unable to write, and his one scheduled
attempt to do a public reading of one of his works, the *Book
of Hours,* he cancelled because he feared he had nothing to
say as a preamble that would either pass the censors or have
any effect on public opinion:

a few years ago, and I might perhaps have still been able to muster
visions which would have resisted even such a time as this, because
my heart was not so worn down then. . . .[36]

The endurance, the acceptance, the achieving of such great afflic-
tions on all sides and by all is wonderful to behold. Greatness comes
to light, perseverance, strength, a standing up to life's *quand-même*
. . . But the fact that such greatness shows itself and stands
the test, can that in any way lessen the anguish over such confusion,
such not knowing which way to turn, over all the sad man-made
aspects of this already provoked fate?—Can it lessen the anguish
that precisely this sheer hopelessness was necessary to compel signs
of courage, devotion, and nobility? While we, the arts, the theater,
evoked nothing from these same people, brought nothing forth
from them, couldn't change anyone.[37]

35. *B. 1914–1921,* 25–26 (dated November 6, 1914).
36. *RMR-MTT,* i, 435 (dated September 6, 1915).
37. *B. 1914–1921,* 49–50 (dated June 28, 1915).

About this time Rilke said to his friend, Katharina Kippenberg:

Art is superfluous. . . . Can art heal wounds, can it take the bitterness away from death? It does not quiet despair, it does not feed the hungry, it does not clothe the freezing.[38]

And in a letter to another friend:

Can anyone hinder or stop [this war]? . . . Why are there not two, three, five, ten who will stand together and cry out in the market-place: "Enough!" and be shot down, and at least have given their lives that it be over; for those who are at the front go down that the atrocity may continue on and on, that no end to the destruction should be forseen. Why is there not *one* who can't bear it any more, who *will not* bear it any more. If he only screamed all one night in the midst of this incredible flag-bedecked city, if he screamed and would not be silenced, who would dare call him a liar?[39]

But, as E. M. Butler has remarked, Rilke was neither saint nor martyr; he was "pure poet, whose mysterious gifts were allied to a childlike irresponsibility. He had urged his compatriots to embrace death in the name of war in August 1914; he now demanded a similar sacrifice from civilians at home for the sake of peace. But that any such self-immolation should be expected of him appeared unthinkable."[40]

His state of mind is shown in the great poem he was able to write in September, "Exposed upon the mountains of the heart," (Appendix, p. 81)[41] and his thoughts on death he expressed best in the wonderful "Death of Moses," (Appendix, p. 82),[42] the first part of which he had brought with him from Paris that summer.

38. Katharina Kippenberg, *Rainer Maria Rilke, Ein Betrag,* 143.
39. *B. 1914–1921* (dated October 10, 1915).
40. *Rilke,* 259.
41. *S.W.* ii, 94.
42. *Ibid.,* 102.

The contents of Rilke's apartment in Paris were auctioned off in April 1915. He described the effect this had on him to Princess Marie:

I go around with the strange feeling, a little like someone who has had a bad fall and got up again unhurt, and yet somehow is not free of the suspicion that a subsequent pain may suddenly break out inside him, and make him scream. Actually I had long ago given it all up and trained myself to test this renunciation on the few things that meant the most to me. It worked, but now I find that despite it all they were still very much there. Now that I know all is gone, a strange fear is stirring in me, as though it were possible to be possessed suddenly by the recollection of some lost object that seems completely indispensible, some small piece of paper perhaps, a picture, a letter in one of the hundred packets of letters, something like that—as though some insignificant thing you loved were lost, and the light fine thread which had joined it to the center of your life were now broken.[43]

In June Duino Castle was bombarded from the sea. Only six shots were fired, but one landed, as Princess Marie later wrote,

upstairs in the rooms above the library. Many trees, even some of the old cypresses are gone. In the lower rose garden—nowhere did the roses bloom so beautifully as there—are soldiers' graves.[44]

Duino was then struck again and again, and finally reduced, as Rilke described it, to "a heap of ruins over countless soldiers' graves."[45] Only the Roman keep and bastions remained standing.[46]

Rilke spent the summer of 1915 in the house of Frau Hertha König who owned Picasso's *Les Saltimbanques*. But

43. *RMR-MTT*, i, 439 (dated September 6, 1915).
44. *Ibid.*, 450 (dated November 10, 1915).
45. *B. 1914–1921* (dated January 21, 1920).
46. The castle was restored after the war to exactly its original state by Princess Marie.

he could not write, and by the end of the summer, he was only more confused and depressed. He wrote to Princess Marie:

A year in Munich has gone by and I have not done much with it. On the contrary I have gone backward in every respect, and how can I do any better now? My heart is so desolate I can't possibly undertake to lead you around in it, in fact chances are it is blocked and impassable.[47]

Then in October he moved to a more inaccessible part of Munich to separate himself from the distractions of the city and the war. Isolation was again the catalyst he needed.

Things which had no particular emphasis earlier on, now come into their own in me; like one early morning . . . when I was reading and full of concentration . . . outside was the park and everything was in harmony with me. It was one of those hours, not at all designed but, so to speak, just saved up, when things drew close and made room for each other—room as untouched as the inside of a rose, an angelic space in which one must keep still. At the time I forgot all about it . . . but now it comes back to me with its own strength and endurance and fills my heart with a clear and imperturbable radiance . . . like lamps, quiet lamps. . . . Since I have been here in this quieter, more remote house, I have remembered many things, lived back and through and beyond them, and then work came very near, in fact it was actually here. . . .[48]

Three days before this he had written the Fourth Elegy. But on November 24, the day after it was finished, he had gone for his first physical examination for the draft (the authorities had worked their way back to those born in 1875). Nora Purtscher-Wydenbruch, in her biography of Rilke, describes how on that day the Austrian artist, Alphons Purtscher (later her husband) who knew Rilke, was working at the Austrian Consulate in Munich:

47. *RMR-MTT*, i, 438 (dated September 6, 1915).
48. *Ibid.*, 452–453 (dated November 26, 1915).

[The] room was full of recruits, who had stripped for their medi-
cal examination and now came, one by one, to his desk where he
handed them their calling-up papers. Unhappy and mostly un-
healthy-looking men—laborers, artisans, and peasants—filed past
him in seemingly unending procession, when he heard the rough
voice of the sergeant-major bellowing: "Rilke!" Involuntarily he
looked up, surprised that anyone else should bear this name. It gave
him a shock when he saw the poet standing before him naked, the
ends of his long mustache hanging down mournfully. The friends
exchanged a glance of silent greeting, and then Alphons Purtscher
affixed the rubber stamp with the two-headed eagle on the docu-
ment condemning the poet to join the Territorial Reserve at
Turnau.[49]

As it turned out, after three weeks of barracks training,
Rilke was transferred to the War Archives Office in Vienna,
where he ended up drawing ruled lines on paper. The Aus-
trian writer, "Sil-Vara," who was assigned the same task de-
scribed Rilke's work:

Industriously he drew vertical and horizontal lines for hours on
end. Sometimes the spaces between the lines were only two milli-
meters wide, but he worked with perfect accuracy and a genuine
humility which bore testimony to his character. Even the severe
geometrical network of pencil lines revealed the aesthetic sense of
its originator, who had almost made a work of art out of it.[50]

In June 1916, through the interceding of friends, he was
released from military service, but for four and a half years
he was able to write virtually nothing.

He went to Switzerland in 1919, still looking for a place
which would allow him the isolation he needed to work on
the elegies. Four were finished and there were fragments of
others, but none had yet been published; they hung over him

49. Nora Purtscher-Wydenbruch, *Rilke, Man and Poet*, 275.
50. *Ibid.*, 278–279.

waiting for the rest to come. He wrote a note to a friend on December 24, 1919:

Years ago, in the winter of 1912, I had for once the stillness, the solitude I need, in fact it lasted four or five months, and it was tremendous. And now I long for one thing only—to take up again the large works begun then . . . but for this the same lack of interruption, the same inwardness is needed, which the mineral has deep inside the mountain when it gathers itself into a crystal. Just yesterday I thought to myself: what can I do to earn this from God? What does the mute creature in the mineral do to earn it.[51]

Toward the end of 1920, a small castle at Berg-am-Irchel near Zurich was offered to Rilke for the winter, and he went there hoping it might prove to be the right place for him. It seemed perfect:

a strong old house made of cut stone, in its present form dating back to the seventeenth century . . . set in a somewhat derelict park in which high trimmed beech alleys border right and left on an unframed *piéce d'eau.* . . . My rooms are large and beautiful, full of old sympathetic things . . . but my heart is pounding away with misgivings, for fear I won't be able to wrest from these utterly agreeable, promising circumstances, the work they now really do allow. I've got to expect it of myself, urgently and stubbornly, after all the distractions and bewilderment of the last few years; . . . if I fail this time . . . then there is nothing that can help me. If a stranger were to walk in, his first words would be: *how* easy it must be to work here! Will I be able? My fear (my cowardice, if you will) is just as great as my job, but this joy is really immense.[52]

The inspiration Rilke needed did not come at Berg, though he did begin there a beautiful elegy on childhood[53] (Appendix, p. 84). He left in May 1921 and moved to Étoy on

51. *B. 1914–1921,* 279–280.
52. *B. 1914–1921,* 338–339 (dated November 25, 1920).
53. *G.W.,* iii, 465.

Lac Léman, to a guest house that had been an old priory. At
the beginning of June, Princess Marie was staying at Rolle,
nearby, and Rilke went there to read her the elegies and
fragments he had written since 1912. She writes in her
Reminiscences:

He confessed, hesitantly at first, then with passionate, anguished
conviction, that he feared he would never finish the Elegies. He
had virtually decided to publish the existing ones and the frag-
ments as they were, since his editor had already waited so long. I
was shocked by this. . . . "The Elegies have got to be completed
—and they will be! I swear to you—only wait, wait. . . . I know
it must come. . . ."[54]

Rilke had been reading Valéry, and in June he made a trans-
lation of *Cimetière Marin.*[55] He remarked several years later
to a friend that at this time he was alone, waiting for his life's
work to come, when one day he read Valéry and knew that his
waiting was over.[56] Valéry had not been able to write any
poetry for twenty-five years, but had then suddenly begun
again. As Rilke put it,

The necessity of artistic expression emerged again when he was
fifty, all the purer in form; and what has come from him since
then is among his most individual and important work.[57]

This encouraged Rilke and allowed him to see an auspicious
side to his own silence. But the impact the other poet had on
him was more far-reaching than this:

The key to the part Valéry played in the release of Rilke's creative
flood lies in the very contrast between them. Rilke was "formed"

54. *Erinnerungen*, 88.
55. *G.W.*, vi, 288.
56. Monique Saint-Hélier (*À Rilke pour Noël*, Berne, 1927) cited in
Purtscher-Wydenbruch, *Rilke, Man and Poet*, 302.
57. *B. aus M.*, 75 (dated December 29, 1921).

in the conceptual sense; the material of his poetry was within him, pressing for escape. The intellectual and intuitive personalities met, and because Valéry approached him from the opposite direction of experience, he was able to effect the clearance in Rilke's creative channel which the latter could not achieve from his own side.[58]

There was also one final change of scene required. Rilke went to Sierre in the Valais to see a house that had been offered to him. It was not what he wanted, but in the window of a hairdresser next to the Hôtel Bellevue he saw a photograph of a thirteenth-century tower "to be let or sold." It turned out to be the Château de Muzot (pronounced Muzotte) which was to be his home for the rest of his life, for a friend first rented and then bought it for him. He said that going there was more like putting on a suit of armor than moving into a house, but the little tower looked out on the Rhone Valley:

So wide and marvelously filled out with smaller elevations all framed by the rim of the huge mountains, that the view continually provides a play of the most seductive changes, like a kind of chess game with the hills. No matter what your vantage point, the arrangement of what you see has a rhythm so astoundingly fresh, it seems like the moment of Creation itself—as if the hills were being shifted and distributed right there before your very eyes . . . the sky takes part in these perspectives from far above and animates them with a spiritual atmosphere, so that the particular way things relate to each other seems at certain hours to have, like in Spain, that same tension we say we feel between the stars of a constellation.[59]

In another place Rilke described the

chapels, and mission crucifixes at every crossroads; slopes striped with vineyards, later on to be amply wreathed with foliage; fruit trees each with its caress of shade and, so perfectly, the single full-

58. K. A. J. Batterby, *Rilke and France*, 148.
59. *RMR-MTT*, ii, 674 (dated July 25, 1921).

grown poplars standing out like the exclamation marks of the place, crying "Here!"[60]

The large room on the upper floor at Muzot, Rilke made into a study. It had a table dated 1700 in it, a small sofa, and soon the small standing desk he always had made when he stayed in a house any length of time, together with a chest, bookshelves, candlesticks, and colored engravings which he found for the room. Von Salis describes being taken through the house by Rilke:

All through his life, the way to the center of his poetic workshop led through the concrete, objective rooms of the place he was living in at the time. Inversely, the struggle to get his surroundings into shape hinted at the coming creative effort. . . . He explained to me as he showed me over Muzot that a poet lacked the tangible raw material, offering resistance and allowing itself to be moulded, which was at the disposal of the sculptor and even of the painter. Poetry was a sublimated art form; it seemed—he said, with a gesture as though trying to draw water with his hands—to run through your fingers. For him, environment and furniture replaced the raw material to some extent, giving him a chance to exercise his creative faculties. . . . As he spoke he lifted the lid of a chest and let me have a glimpse of piles of letters in packets, manuscripts and books arranged in the most wonderful order. This orderliness, this precision with regard to the smallest and least important matters, was one of the most striking features about Rainer Maria's way of life. . . .[61]

Rilke once wrote

that for each situation you want to communicate there is only one expression that will really work—and in this task, grace comes to your help to let you be so divinely exact. In life it is effort that can make us human, or rather—alas—the slightest approach to being human. But anyone who knows that heavenly precision which

60. *B. aus M.*, 45 (dated November 26, 1921).
61. *Rainer Maria Rilke, The Years in Switzerland*, 125–126.

comes to us from the inner core of art, is tormented by having always to remain *à peu près* in so many fields of endeavor, not to say bungling, or disfiguring. . . .[62]

Von Salis remembers that

Almost enviously [Rilke] would see the boy standing outside the door every morning at a quarter past seven "with wonderful milk and butter," or watch him "working away at the saw like a hero"[63]

and only wish he were half so efficient.

He spent that first winter at Muzot cultivating the solitude he needed. He even turned down the offer of a dog because he felt a relationship might develop which would prove too much of a distraction.

To "pull down" so to speak, the hindrances of the war years, to loosen stone after stone from the wall that encircled me and seemed to cut me off from the past no less than from all that might be yet to come—that is still my modest assignment.[64]

When I look into my conscience I see only one law; it stubbornly commands me to lock myself up in myself, and in one stretch to finish this task that was dictated to me at the center of my heart. I am obeying—for you know it's true, in coming here I wanted only that, and I have no right to alter the course my will has taken, until I have completed this act of sacrifice and obedience.[65]

May the "work" really come about then, or at least the inner state of mind that corresponds to it in intensity and purity . . . and then the solitude in my old tower will not have been unimportant, one way or another.[66]

62. Previously unpublished letter to Mme. Nanny Wunderly-Volkart, dated July 30, 1921, quoted in von Salis, *op. cit.*, German edition, 104.
63. *Op. cit.*, 126–127.
64. *B. aus M.*, 95 (dated January 28, 1922).
65. *Ibid.*, 15 (n.d.).
66. *Ibid.*, 47–48 (dated November 26, 1921).

This last was written to Rilke's friend, Gertrud Ouckama Knoop. At the end of the letter he spoke of her daughter, Wera, who had been a childhood playmate of his own daughter, Ruth, and had died two years before at only nineteen. He asked her mother to tell him about her death, which she did in a letter that reached him on January 1, 1922, and her description of Wera filled him with a great sense of obligation to the memory of the dead girl. It came as a kind of challenge to create something for her. E. M. Butler writes that it dislodged a kind of keystone in him and

gradually the movement spread to other tightly wedged and stationary blocks of inert inspiration. Imperceptibly they gave way, began to float and yielded to the current; gently at first and then rapidly swept along by the river which had not been able to dislodge them all those weary years.[67]

On February 2, he began to write, not the Elegies as he had hoped, but the first sequence of the *Sonnets to Orpheus*. They were completed by February 5 and he sent them to Frau Ouckama Knoop on February 7:

In a few utterly gripping days, when I had actually intended to take up other work, these sonnets have been given to me. You will realize at first glance why you must be the first to have them. For as broken up as the reference [to Wera] is . . . it dominated and set in motion the entire sequence and penetrated its irresistible, heart-wrenching emergence, although so secretly that I only gradually perceived it.[68]

But then immediately following the *Sonnets to Orpheus* the Elegies began to come; the Seventh on February 7, and the Sixth, Eighth, Ninth, and the *Gegen-strophen* (Appendix, p. 77)[69] (which stood for a while as the Fifth) by

67. *Rilke*, 312.
68 *B. aus M.*, 98.
69. *G.W.*, iii, 457 (begun in 1912).

February 9. The Seventh needed only a rewording of its last six lines, and this was done on February 26. The Eighth which was written on February 7–8 needed no revision.

On the evening of February 9 Rilke went to the Sierre post office to send a wire (5:10 P.M.) to Frau Wunderly telling her that seven elegies were now complete, "at all events, the most important ones. Joy and miracle."[70] He wrote to her the next morning that on his way back from the post office "the Eighth and Ninth finished and formed themselves around smaller and larger earlier fragments."[71] But as no such fragments have ever been found for the Eighth Elegy, it has been suggested, and agreed upon by Rilke's present editors, that he was in fact referring to the *Sixth* and Ninth Elegies which were the "eighth and ninth" to be *completed* (including the *Gegen-strophen*) and for both of which fragments are known to have existed. The "larger" of these was the first thirty-one lines of the Sixth Elegy written in Spain in 1913, together with its final three lines dating from that same year in Paris. Of the Ninth Elegy only lines one to the first half of six, and seventy-seven to seventy-nine existed, dating from March 1912.

So it was the remaining eleven lines of the Sixth and the major part of the Ninth Elegy that Rilke wrote down when he returned home from the Sierre post office that winter night, February 9, 1922. Before he went to bed he wrote to Anton Kippenberg:

it is late, and I can scarcely hold the pen any more after some days of tremendous obedience to the spirit—still I must . . . must tell you today, now, before I try to get some sleep:
    I am over the hill!
Finally! The "Elegies" are here. And can be published this year

70. von Salis, *op. cit.*, 141.
71. *Ibid.*, previously unpublished letter.

(or whenever you see fit). Nine long ones, in about the same scale that you already know. . . .

So

Dear friend, now at last I will be able to breathe a sigh of relief and turn to more manageable things. For this was more than life-size—I've been groaning day and night, like that time at Duino—but even after that struggle, I never knew that *such* a storm out of heart and spirit could come driving over me. Or that it could be survived! Survived. Enough, it is here.

I went out into the cold moonlight and stroked my little Muzot like a great animal—the old walls that yielded it all to me. And the ruined walls of Duino.

The whole cycle will be called:

The Duino Elegies![72]

That same evening the postman had brought some white hyacinths, but with no card to say who had sent them.

In his letter the following morning to Frau Wunderly Rilke wrote:

That I was still permitted to experience *this* . . . experience *being* it. . . . I would not have held out one day longer (like that time at Duino, only worse), all tissue and ligature in me cracked in the storm. . . . I must be well made to have withstood it.

God grant me only quiet, peaceful tasks now, human ones, no more of these that exceed all common, warranted strength.

It is done, done!

The blood cycle, the legendary cycle of ten (ten!) strange years has come to an end. I feel now as if my heart were mutilated by this thing not being there any more! This thing that now exists on its own.[73]

On February 11, he finished the Tenth Elegy. The first version of the poem (Appendix, p. 69) had been completed

72. *Br. Verleger*, ii, 409–410.
73. von Salis, *op. cit.*, German edition, 117–118, previously unpublished letter.

in the fall of 1913, but of this he now kept only the first fifteen lines which dated from Duino, 1912. It is possible of course that he had worked on the poem in the meantime; in a letter undated but assigned by his editors to December 1921, he speaks of the research he had been doing on the catkins which appear toward the end of the Elegy. (See notes on lines 107–108 of the Tenth Elegy, p. 73.) It is not known therefore, just how much of it was actually written on February 11.

That same day, he wrote to Princess Marie:

At last
    Princess,
        at last, the blessed, how blessed day when I can announce to you the completion—so far as I can see—of the
        Elegies
        Ten!
    From the last, large one (the opening lines begun, long ago at Duino . . .) from this last one which was intended even then to be the *last*,—from this—my hand is still trembling! Just now, Saturday, the *eleventh*, at six o'clock in the evening, it is done!—
    All in a few days, it was an unspeakable storm, a hurricane in the spirit . . . I never even thought of eating, God knows who fed me.
        But now *it is*. Is. Is.
            Amen.
I have survived for this purpose, come through everything. Through everything. And this was really what was needed. *Only* this. . . . The whole of it is *yours*, Princess; how could it help being yours! It will be called:
    The Duino Elegies
In the book (for I cannot give you what has belonged to you from the beginning) there will be no dedication, I think, but only:
    The property of . . .
P.S. Please, dear Princess, don't think it a subterfuge on the part of my laziness, when I tell you why I am not sending you the new *Elegies* now: I would be jealous of your reading them. I

feel it should definitely be I who *first* reads them to you. When? Soon now, I hope.[74]

Rilke sent Frau Wunderly a fair copy of the Elegies (containing as yet the original Fifth) written into a little parchment book which he had found at Soglio in 1919, when he first came to Switzerland. It was *"mal habillé,"* he told her, but:

Napoleon also, on the day of one of his great victories didn't want to diminish its glory by bothering vainly to get all dressed up! But truthfully, I say this with all my heart, this little book from Soglio shines and is precious:
    it was not mine

                                        ever
I was never more humble, never more on my knees:
    oh
    infinitely!

                              R.[75]

On February 14, Rilke wrote an eleventh elegy which replaced the *Gegen-strophen* as the Fifth Elegy, because it better suited the cycle; then on the three following days, came the second series of *Sonnets to Orpheus,* comprising twenty-nine poems. He described the writing of the Fifth Elegy as a "radiant after-storm."[76] It is dedicated to Frau Hertha König whose Picasso, *Les Saltimbanques,* had so impressed him when he stayed at her house in Munich during the summer of 1915. This painting was once thought to be the direct source of the Elegy; there are, however, a number of discrepancies between Picasso's acrobats and Rilke's. A letter Rilke wrote to a Czechoslovak sculptress, Dora Heidrich, in 1907 describes the acrobats he saw in Paris at that

74. *RMR-MTT*, ii, 697–699.

75. von Salis, *op. cit.*, 143, previously unpublished letter (dated February 12, 1922).

76. *RMR-LAS*, 468.

time, and the details of the account are closer to the Elegy than are those in the painting. Dieter Bassermann writes that:

It is now possible to ascertain (and correct) the relationship of the Picasso painting . . . to the Elegy; that it was not the occasion and source of the poem, as it was generally taken to be before the discovery of the letter. . . . [The *saltimbanques* of Rilke's early Paris period] were the ingredients from which . . . the Elegy emerged.[77]

A longer version of the Paris experience found in one of Rilke's notebooks, dated the same day as the letter to Dora Heidrich and from which the description in the letter was no doubt taken, has since been published:

In front of the Luxembourg Gardens, near the Pantheon, Père Rollin and his troupe have spread themselves out. The same carpet is lying there, the same overcoats, thick winter coats, taken off and piled on a chair, leaving just enough room for the little son, the old man's grandson, to come and sit down now and then during intervals. He still needs to, he is only a beginner they say, and those headlong leaps to the ground out of high somersaults make his feet sore. He has a large face that can take a swarm of tears, but often they hold back inside the rim of his swollen eyes. Then he has to carry his head carefully, like a cup that is full to the brim. Nevertheless, he is not depressed; on the contrary, he wouldn't even pay any attention to it, if that were possible; it is simply the pain of tears that one must tolerate. With time it gets easier and finally it goes away. His father has long since forgotten what it was like, and his grandfather forgot over sixty years ago, otherwise he would not have become so famous. But look, Père Rollin, who has become so famous at all the fairs, he doesn't "work" any more. He doesn't swing the huge weights any more and though he was once the most eloquent of all, he says nothing now. He has been transferred to beating the drum. He stands around patiently with his too far-gone athlete's face, its features sagging in loose con-

77. Dieter Bassermann, *Der Späte Rilke*, 417.

fusion, as if a weight had been hung on each of them, stretching it. Dressed plainly, a sky-blue knitted cravat around his colossal neck, he has retired at the peak of his genuine fame, in this coat, into this humble spot—on which, no glance ever falls. But anyone among these young people who has ever seen him, knows that in those sleeves are the famous muscles hidden away, whose slightest touch used to bring the weights springing up; how could anyone forget such a masterpiece. And so he says a few words to the person next to him, shows him where to look, and then the old man feels their glance on him, lost in thought as he is, vague and respectful. That strength is still there, young folks, he says to himself; not handy any more, but that's the whole point: it's gone into the roots—it's still there somewhere, the whole lot of it. But it is far too much, on the whole, for beating a drum. He attacks it, beats it much too often. And his son-in-law has to whistle to him about it and give him a warning look just when he is in the middle of one of his tirades. The old man stops, frightened; he tries to excuse himself with his heavy shoulders and ceremoniously put his other foot forward. But already he has to be whistled down again. The Devil! Père! Père Rollin! He's already drumming again. He scarcely knows it. He could go on drumming forever and on no account are they to think that he might become tired. But there, his daughter is speaking to him; quick on the trigger and sturdy, consistently all there and with more wit than any of the others. By and large it's she who holds things together, and it's a joy to behold. The son-in-law works well, to be sure—no one can deny that, and he likes his work, it's a part of him. But one feels she has it in her blood. This is something you have to be born to. She's ready! Music, she cries. And the old man beats away at his drum like fourteen drummers. Père Rollin, hey, Père Rollin, calls one of the spectators, and steps right up, recognizing him. But the old man only incidentally nods to him. The drumming is a point of honor with him and he takes it seriously.[78]

This is the scene Rilke set in the precise lines of the Fifth Elegy, these loving descriptions made eighteen years before,

78. *S.W.*, vi, 1137–1139.

and each character he has delineated in just its own man-
ner. Rilke's one-time secretary, Marga Wertheimer, wrote
that often

Rilke spoke of the traveling circus people who came to Paris every
year, always at the same season; and he made a point of talking
to them, following the lives and the development of the circus
family, especially of the one daughter.[79]

He said in a letter that the *saltimbanques*

ever since the earliest time in Paris concerned me so absolutely,
and have enlisted me ever since.[80]

With the Fifth Elegy and the second series of *Sonnets to
Orpheus* the rush of inspiration was over, having lasted nine-
teen days. Then a reaction set in as he had expected it would:

When you have been hurled up you have to fall somewhere. But
after all, I can fall into spring which is already nearly here. And
then, since I have been granted patience, the long patience to reach
what is now here—why shouldn't I be able to manage a little near-
patience to get me through some blue days. And finally shouldn't
I be grateful (I've just now been more so than ever before) and
let that outweigh everything that is annoying and confusing these
days.[81]

He wrote that February 26, the last Sunday of the month,

was from early to late rightly named for the sun, (it shone almost
like summer here, right down into the soil of this landscape it
knows it can trust). And when I went into my study there were
early roses there, and downstairs, on the breakfast table—for no
apparent reason . . . a dough-cake and a little bowl with the first

79. *Arbeitsstunden mit R.M.R.*, 43–44, cited by Heerikhuizen, *op. cit.*,
327.
80. *RMR-LAS*, 469 (dated February 19, 1922).
81. *Ibid.*

cowslips from our fields, still shaky and short in the stem, but already quite happy.[82]

They had been carefully placed there by Rilke's housekeeper, Frida, of whom he wrote that she

bravely stood her ground those days when Muzot was riding the high sea of the spirit . . . providing for me and fearless while I was up here shouting terrible cries of command, receiving signals from outer space, and roaring out my welcoming salvos to them![83]

That spring with the burden of the Elegies gone, Rilke was at last free to accept the simple chores and impressions of ordinary life again. When Princess Marie came in June to hear the *Elegies*, she found

a transformed man, a radiantly happy man. . . . On the morning of June 7, I was at Muzot. Intimate, diminutive, low-ceilinged rooms with old furniture—flowers, masses of flowers everywhere, including five-petalled, flame-colored roses. A St. Francis kneeling, a few simple engravings on the wall, an earthenware stove made in the valley. . . . Then we went up to his study—a room full of books, full of devotion. . . .
And finally, standing at his desk as he was in the habit of doing, he began to read. . . . That morning he read the first seven, and in the afternoon the last three. . . .[84]

Rilke was then only forty-seven, but all his important work was completed. By the end of the year he had contracted leukemia, and in four and a half years he died.

---

82. *Ibid.*, 472 (dated February 27, 1922).
83. von Salis, *op. cit.*, German edition, previously unpublished letter (dated February 15, 1922).
84. *Op. cit.*, 93–94.

The First Elegy

Who, if I cried, would hear me from the order
of Angels? And even if one suddenly held me
to his heart: I would dissolve there from
his stronger presence. For beauty is only
5   the beginning of a terror we can just barely endure,
and what we so admire is its calm
disdaining to destroy us. Every Angel brings terror.
So I withhold myself and keep back the lure
of my dark sobbing. Oh, who is there
10 to prevail upon? Neither Angels nor men,
and already the ingenious beasts are aware
that we are not reliably at home
in our interpreted world. There remains for us, perhaps
a tree standing somewhere on its slope, that we may
15 see again each day; yesterday's walk remains
and the spoiled affection of a habit
which liked being with us, and so stayed and never departed.
Oh, and the night, night when the wind full of world space
consumes our features—for whom would she not stay on,
20 that longed for, gently deceiving one who

painfully awaits the separate heart. Is she easier for lovers?
Alas, they only conceal with each other their fate.
Do you *still* not understand? Fling the emptiness out from
          your arms
into the spaces we breathe: maybe the birds will
25   feel the thinner air with a more inward flight.

Yes, the springtime did need you. Many stars
demanded that you sense them. A wave
long since gone by lifted itself toward you,
or when you passed a window that was open, a violin
30   gave itself up. All this was a charge.
But did you complete it? Were you not always
distracted with expectation, as though this were
but announcing someone you could love? (Where would you
have concealed her, with those strange heavy thoughts
35   going in and out of you, often lasting into the night.)
When longing overcomes you, sing of the Lovers; their
famous feeling is not immortal enough.
Those you nearly envied, those forsaken whom you found
so much more loving than requited lovers. Begin
40   again, always anew, your ever inadequate praising;
Think: the hero lasts on, and even his downfall
was a pretext for existing, a final birth.
But lovers are drawn by exhausted Nature back
into herself, as though there were not strength enough
45   to achieve them a second time. Have you remembered
well enough Gaspara Stampa; that any girl deserted
by her lover, from this exalted example
might feel: that I might be like her?
Should not this ancient pain at last produce in us
50   more fruit? Is it not time that our loving
freed us from our beloved and we, trembling, endured;

as the arrow endures the string that, gathered to leap forth,
it may be *more* than itself. For staying is nowhere.

Voices, voices. Hear my heart, as before this
55 only saints have heard: till the giant call
plucked them from the ground; and yet
impossible ones, they went on kneeling, heedless:
such was their hearing. Not that you could endure
the voice of *God*—far from it. But mark the breathing,
60 the unbroken word that builds itself out of silence.
It rustles toward you now from those youthful dead.
Always in Rome and Naples wherever you stepped
into a church, did not their fate calmly address you?
Or some raised inscription deliver you its charge,
65 as recently the tablet in Santa Maria Formosa?
What they require of me? that gently I take off
the look of suffered wrong, which often a little
hinders the pure movement of their spirits.

True, it is strange to live no longer on earth,
70 and to practice no longer customs scarcely acquired;
roses, and other expressly promising things,
not to give them the meaning of human future;
what in endlessly anxious hands one used to be,
to be this no more, and even one's own name
75 to lay aside, like a toy that is broken.
Strange, not to go on with one's wishes. Strange
to see all relations go loosely
fluttering in space. And it is tiresome to be dead
and full of retrieving, so that one must sense
80 traces of eternity by degrees.—But all the living
mistakenly draw too sharp distinctions.
Angels (one says) often are not sure if they

move among living or dead. The eternal torrent
hurls all ages along through both realms
85   forever, and sounds above them in both.

Finally, the ones gone early away, they do not need us
any more. One is gently weaned from the earth
even as we gently turn from our mother's breasts.
But we who need such great secrets, for whom out of sorrow
90   so often blessed progress springs—*could* we exist
         without them?
Is the tale to no purpose, that once in mourning for Linos
the first daring music pierced through
that rigid bleakness: that only in the startled space which
         suddenly
an almost godlike youth abandoned, the Void
95   came into that vibration which now transports us and
         comforts and helps.

The Second Elegy

Every Angel brings terror. And yet, woe is me,
my song calls upon you, near-deadly birds of the soul,
knowing who you are. Where have the days of Tobias gone
when one supremely shining stood in a simple doorway,
5 disguised a little for the journey and no longer frightening;
(young to the young one as he curiously peered out.)
Should the archangel, the perilous one, behind the stars
take a single step downward and toward us, our own
surging hearts would slay us. Who are you?

10 Early children of luck, you favorites of the world,
mountain ranges, ridges morning-red
of all creation,—pollen of blossoming deity,
hinges of light, passages, stairways, thrones,
spaces of being, shields made of rapture, tumults
15 of unbridled enchantment and suddenly, by themselves,
mirrors: each drawing back into its countenance again
its own outstreamed beauty.

For we, where we feel, evaporate; oh we
breathe ourselves out and beyond; hot ember to ember

20 we yield a weakening scent. Someone may say to us:
"you get into my blood, the room, the spring
is full of you" . . . No use, he cannot hold us;
we vanish in him and around him. And those who are fair,
oh, who shall hold them back? Incessantly, semblance
25 rises up in their faces and goes. Like dew on spring grass
there lifts from us all that we are, as heat lifts
from a steaming dish. O smile, where are you going?
      O upturned gaze:
new, warm, disappearing wave of the heart—
it grieves me: but we *are* this. The space
30 in which we have dissolved—does it taste of us? Do Angels
intercept what from themselves alone has streamed,
or, at times, is there as well some inadvertent trace
of our existence? Are we in their lineaments involved
no more than in a pregnant woman's face there is
35 that look of vagueness? It goes unnoticed in the whirl
of her returning to herself. (Why should she notice?)

Lovers, if they but knew, could in the night air
speak wonderful things. For it seems that all things
conceal us. Look, the trees *exist;* and the houses
40 we live in—still stand. But we pass them by
like an exchange of breath.
And all is in agreement to ignore us; half as shame, perhaps
and half as ineffable hope.

Lovers, you that are satisfied with each other, I question you
45 about ourselves. You grasp each other. But have you proof?
For I have found my hands
become aware of each other, my out-worn face
spare itself within them. This brings some slight
sensation. But who from this alone would dare *exist?*

50 You though, that in the other's ecstasy increase
    till he is overcome and pleads, "No *more*"—
    you that beneath each other's hands
    become, like vintage years, more ample;
    you that lapse at times, but only when the other
55 takes the upper hand, I ask you about ourselves. I know
    you touch so blissfully each other, because caressing lingers,
    because the place you tender ones have covered
    does not vanish; because you can perceive
    the pure duration there. From an embrace you find
60 almost the promise of eternity. And yet when that first
    frightening encounter is endured, and longing at the window,
    and the first walk you took together, through the garden
    only *once*: Lovers, *are* you still this? When to each
    other's lips you lift and begin—: drink unto drink:
65 how strangely the drinker then eludes his act.

    Did it not astound you, on Attic steles—
    the caution of human gesture? were not love and farewell
    on shoulders there so lightly laid, as if they were
    made of other stuff than we? Recall the hands—
70 how they rest weightless, though in the torsos there is force.
    Those restrained ones knew: that we get only so far:
    that ours is only *so* to touch each other; the gods can
    press more strongly on us. But that is the concern of the gods.

    Could we as well but find some pure, contained
75 and human, our own small piece of orchard
    between river and rock. For our heart transcends us now
    as with those others. And we can gaze no longer after it
    into pictures which gentle it, or in godlike bodies
    where it has found that greater control.

The Third Elegy

It is one thing to sing the beloved. Another, alas,
that obscure, guilty river-god of the blood.
Only from a distance known to her, what can her lover
himself tell of that lord of all lust, who often out of
5   this lonely one, and before the girl could comfort him,
      often as if
she *were* not, oh, streaming from what unknowable—
heaved up his godhead, calling the night to endless riot.
O Neptune of the blood, O his frightening trident,
O the dark wind out of his breast in the wound shell!
10   Listen, how the night grows cavernous, hollow sounding.
      You stars,
does not this lover's desire for the face of his beloved
descend from you? Has he not learned his insight
into her pure look from your pure points of light?

It was not you, alas, and not his mother
15   that bent this arch of longing on his brow.
Not toward you, maiden holding him, not toward you
have his lips curved with more fruitful line. Do you really
      think

your slight approach could so convulse him,
you that wander like a morning breeze?
20 True, you startled his heart, but more ancient terrors
surged in him with your offending touch. Call him . . .
you can't quite draw him from that dark acquaintance.
He *wills*, he escapes, and being lightened, grows accustomed
to your covert heart; takes and there begins himself.
25 But did he ever begin himself?
Mother, *you* made him small; you once began him.
He was new with you; you bent the friendly world
over his new eyes and warded off strangeness.
Oh where are those years when simply with your slender form
30 you stood between him and this surging chaos?
So you hid much from him. Your presence could disarm
at night the suspect room, and from your full heart's refuge
a human space poured into his own night space.
Not there in darkness did you set your lamp,
35 no, but in your nearer being, and it shown as though
out of friendship; nowhere a creaking you could not smile
       away
as if you knew just *when* the floor would so behave . . .
He listened and grew calm. All this your coming
quietly availed. Behind the cupboard
40 stepped his tall mantled fate, and disarranged,
his restless future slid into long curtain folds.

And he, how he lay, the lightened one, beneath
his drowsing lids, dissolving the sweetness
of your light form in the first foretaste of sleep—
45 *seemed* like one watched over . . . but *inside,* who could
ward off, divert in him the tide of his origin?
Oh, there *was* no caution in that sleeping child; sleeping,
but also dreaming, fevered: how he ventured in.

He, the new one, shying off, how he was ensnared
50 by the grasping tendrils of interior events already
tangled into network, into choking undergrowth, into
stalking animal forms. And how he surrendered—And loved.
Loved his interior world, his inner wildness,
this primal forest in whose mute fallen ruins
55 light-green his heart was standing. Loved. And left,
went out from his own roots into vast beginning,
where his scant birth already was surpassed. Loving,
he sank into the older blood, into ravines
where the frightful lay, still sated with his fathers.
60 And everything dreadful knew him, winked, seemed well
        informed.
The horrible smiled at him . . . Seldom, mother,
with such tenderness had you smiled at him. And how
could he not love what smiled at him? Before you
had he loved it: when you carried him, it was dissolved
65 in the water that lightened the springing seed.

Look, we do not love like flowers, stemming
from a single year; but when we love
a sap beyond all memory lifts in our arms. O girl,
just *this:* that we *inside* ourselves have loved not one
70 still in the future, but a countless fermentation; not one child,
but fathers, lying in our soil like mountain ruins;
but the dried-up river bed of former mothers—
but all that soundless landscape
under its clear-skied or clouded misfortune:
75 *this,* girl, was there before you.

And yourself, how could you know you would awaken that
fore-time in your lover. What feelings

surged up from beings no longer here. What
women hated you. What sinister men
80 did you rouse in his young veins? Dead
children reached for you. . . . Oh, gently, gently,
do in love for him each day some reliable task,—lead him
near to the garden, give him the heavy
weight of night . . . . . .
                              Don't let him go . . . . . .

The Fourth Elegy

O trees of life, when does your winter come?
We are not one, not made aware
like migratory birds. Late and out of season
we suddenly force ourselves upon the winds
5 and fall into the indifferent pond. Flowering
and fading we apprehend together.
And somewhere lions still move, so long magnificent
they recognize no weakness in themselves.

But we, while set entirely on one thing,
10 already feel the price of others. Hostility
is second nature to us. Do not lovers always
overreach the limits of each other's lives,
having promised distance, chase and home.
Then in the sketchwork of the moment
15 painfully a background is prepared as contrast,
to help us see; for they are very clear
with us. We do not know the contour
of our feeling, but only what informs it from outside.
Who has not sat before the curtain of his heart, frightened?

20   Until it opened on a scene of parting.
      Not hard to understand. The familiar garden,
      and swaying slightly: then the dancer made his entrance.
      Not *him*. Enough. However gracefully he move
      he is disguised, and turns into a tradesman
25   who goes into his house through the kitchen door.
      I do not want these half-filled masks,
      but rather, the doll. It is solid. I can endure
      the wire and the rags for dress,
      the face no more than surface. Here. I'm waiting.
30   And if the lamps go out and I am told
      "No more,"—if from the stage
      emptiness come toward me in the grey draft;
      if none of my silent forbears
      will sit beside me any more, no woman,
35   not even the boy with the brown bent eye:
      even then, I'll stay. One can always watch.

      Am I not right? Father, you for whom
      this life of mine had such a bitter taste;
      that first troubled distillation of my *must*,
40   as I grew older yet you kept on tasting,
      and with an alien future's aftertaste concerned,
      you tried my clever gaze;—
      you that since your death, in my hope
      have feared for me, within me,
45   and that serenity the dead may claim, realms
      of serenity, surrendered it for my tiny bit of fate,—
      am I not right? And you, am I not right,
      you that loved me for my first small impulse
      of love toward you, from which I always turned:
50   because it seemed, the space in your eyes
      even while I loved it, changed into world-space
      in which you were no more . . . : when I feel like

waiting before the puppet stage, no,
gazing within, so deeply that to counter-weigh
55 my sight in the end, an angel
must appear as player, plucking up the rags?
Angel and doll: then finally there is a play.
Then there is joined what we must always sever
while we are there. Then can arise
60 out of our seasons, the cycle
of the whole procession. Over and beyond us then
will the angel play. Look, the dying—
should they not suspect how full of pretense
our performance is. Here where
65 nothing is itself. O childhood hours
when behind the figures meeting us was more
than the past, and before us was not the future.
We were growing, often crowding into years ahead
half for love of some
70 whose grown-up-ness, we knew, was all they had.
And when we were within our solitude,
delighted with sheer duration, we stood there
in the between-spaces between the world and our toys,
upon a place which from the earliest beginning
75 had been established for a pure event.

Who will present a child just as he stands? Who will
set him in his stars, and give the measure of distance
into his hand? Who will make the death of a child
out of grey bread that grows hard,—or leave it
80 there within his round mouth like the core
of an enticing apple? . . . Murderers' thoughts
are easily recognized. But this: Death, the whole of death,
and even when our life has not *begun*,
to contain it gently and without resentment:
85 this lies beyond description.

The Fifth Elegy

But tell me who these *are*, these travelling men
even more fugitive than we ourselves,
compelled from birth, oh for *whose, whose,* sake
wrung by some never satiate will?
5   But it wrings them, bends them, flails, devours them,
hurls and catches them; as from oiled
and polished air they fall again
upon the threadbare carpet their
eternal leaping has worn thin. Carpet
10 lost in space, and laid on
like a plaster where the sky above the outskirts
had scraped the earth.
                                        And scarcely there,
but upright, manifest: like the large initials
15 of *Standing-there* . . . , but then, already
by that constantly returning grasp, the strongest men
are rolled again in jest, as once by August the Strong
a tin plate at his table.

But oh, around this
20 center, blooms and sheds

the rose of onlooking. Around this pestle,
this pistil struck by its own pollen,
fertilized again
for the sham-fruit of the pain
25   they never recognized, and gleaming with
the slightly-appearing-to-smile of thin-surfaced pain.

There the wrinkled, sagging strong man,
the old one, only drumming now;
shrivelled up inside his great skin as though
30   it once contained *two* men, but one now
lay in the churchyard, and he had outlasted him,
deaf and often, in his widowed skin,
a little bit confused.

But the young one, the man, as though he were
35   the offspring of a neck and of a nun: taut and vigorously
filled with muscle and simplicity.

O you
that during one drawn-out recovery
received a small sorrow
40   like a plaything . . . . .

You that with the impact
which only fruit can know, fall
unripe each day a hundred times from that tree
of jointly engendered movement, (tree swifter than water
45   that in a few minutes has its autumn, spring and summer)—
fall and rebound on the grave:
sometimes in half pauses, a loving look would
rise in your face toward your seldom
tender mother; then lose itself on your body

50   whose surface would consume that shy
        and scarcely attempted expression . . . And again
        the man's hands clap for the leap; and before
        a pain close to your ever-racing heart
        becomes distinct, your footsole's burning
55   forestalls this source, chasing fast
        into your eyes a few sharp mortal tears.
        And yet, blindly,
        the smile . . . . .

        Angel! Take it, pluck that small-flowered healing herb!
60   Bring a vase and keep it! Set it with those joys
        as yet not open to us; praise it on a lovely urn
        with soaring, blossoming inscription:
                                "*Subrisio Saltat.*"

        Then you, lovely one,
65   whom the most tempting joys
        silently overpass. Perhaps
        the fringes of your dress are happy in your stead, or
        covering your young tight breasts
        the green metallic silk feels
70   endlessly indulged, in need of nothing.
        You,
        on trembling balance scales, forever changing,
        cool like laid-out market fruit,
        held public from the shoulders.

75   Oh *where* is that place—I bear it in my heart—
        where still they *could* not, still
        they fell apart like mating animals
        not rightly paired;—
        where still the weights are heavy;

80   still their vainly twirling sticks
      can let the hoops go
      staggering off . . . . .

      For in this toilsome nowhere, suddenly
      that untold place where clear Too-little
85   incomprehensively is transformed,—swings round
      into that empty Too-much.
      Where the many-digited account
      is balanced numberless.

      Squares, o square in Paris, endless showplace,
90   where the modiste, *Madame Lamort,*
      winds and coils the unquiet ways of the world
      like endless ribbons, and from her colored bows
      contrives new flowers, frills, cockades, and artificial
      fruits, all falsely dyed,—for the cheap
95   winter-hats of fate.
     . . . .

      Angel! Could there be a place we have not known, and there
      on an ineffable carpet, lovers revealed all that here
      they can never accomplish, the daring
100 high figures of the heart's flight,
      their towers made of pleasure, ladders
      leaning only on each other where there was never
      ground, and swaying,—and *could* it be
      before those rings of spectators, the countless silent dead,
105 would they not fling their last, their always kept back, always
      hidden and unknown to us, forever valid
      coins of happiness before that pair whose smile
      at last was true, out on the quietened
      carpet?

The Sixth Elegy

Fig tree, for how long now have I found meaning
in the way you almost entirely neglect to bloom,
and then into the season-purposed fruit
uncelebrated, urge your purest secret.
5 Like a fountain's pipe, the sap drives through the arching
       bough
downward and on, and it springs out of sleep,
almost not waking, in the joy of its sweetest achievement,
See: like the God into the swan.
                    . . . . . But we still linger,
10 Ah, our pride is in blooming, and to the delayed core
of our final fruit we come already betrayed.
In a few there stems so sharply the impulse to action
that they stand already glowing in their fullness of heart
when like a softened night-air the temptation to flower
15 touches the youth of their mouths and of their eyelids.
Heroes perhaps, and the ones called early away,
those in whom gardening death has twisted the veins awry,
these plunge on ahead, with their own laughter
beforehand, like that charging span in the lightly
20 chiseled reliefs of Karnak the victorious king.

Strangely near is the hero to the young dead. Survival
does not concern him. Ascent is his existence; continually
he impels himself on and enters the changed constellation
of his constant danger; there few could find him. But
25 what shrouds us in silence, the sudden and impassioned Fate
sings him into the storm of its surging world.
None do I hear that are like him. All at once goes through me,
streaming upon the air, his darkened tone.

Then how gladly I'd hide myself from the yearning.
    Oh were I,
30 were I a boy and dared to become it, to sit
 propped on the arms of my future, reading of Samson,
 how his mother bore nothing at first and then everything.

Was he not hero in you already, O mother;
began not there within you his masterful choice?
35 Thousands brewed in your womb and willed to become *him*,
but look: he seized and passed over, chose and prevailed.
And if he broke columns apart, it was when he tore
out of the world of your limbs to this narrower world
where he further chose and prevailed. O mothers of heroes,
40 deep sources of raging streams! You ravines whereinto
high from the heart's rim, lamenting
maidens already have fallen, to be offered to the sons.

For whenever the hero stormed through the stations of love,
each lifted him onward, each heartbeat that meant him;
45 and already turned away,
 he stood at the end of the smiles, an alien.

The Seventh Elegy

Wooing no more, not wooing, O outgrown voice
shall be the intent of your cry; though it sound as pure as
    the bird's
when the soaring season uplifts him, almost forgetting
that he's a small anxious thing, and not just the single heart
5 that she hurls toward brightness, into the intimate heavens.
     Like him
no less would you be wooing some still invisible
silent love, in whose waking
an answer kindled, and warmed itself over the listening,
to your rising passion's flame, the glowing reflection.
10 O and the Spring would accept it—, there is no scene
but would bear the note of annunciation. First the small
questioning treble, then the day's pure affirmation
compasses all about with a climbing calm.
Then to the stairs, the call-stairs up to the dreamed-of
15 temple of the future—; then the trill, the fountain,
whose starting spray is already teased into falling
by the promise of play . . . And before it all, the Summer.
Not only all the dawns of Summer, not only

the way they transpose into day and brighten before light,
20 not only the days, so tender in the flowers, and above
about the tall tree-patterns, stark and forceful.
Not only the devotion of these unfolded powers,
not only the woodpaths, the meadows at evening,
not only after late thunder, the breathing freshness,
25 not only the nearing of sleep and its insight, evenings . . .
but the nights! but the high summer nights,
but the stars, the stars of the earth.
O to be dead and unendingly know them,
all the stars, for then how, how ever to forget them.

30 Look, I have called to my lover, but not only *she*
would come . . . out of the weakened graves
girls would gather and stand . . . For how could I limit it,
the call given out? The sunken ones always
seek the earth again. You children, one present
35 thing grasped here is valid for many.
Do not believe Fate to be more than the wisdom of childhood;
for how often you'd outdistance your beloved, panting,
panting for a blessed run straight into the open.

To be present is glorious. You knew it, even *you*
40 girls, who seemingly went without, sank under, in the
saddest streets of the cities, festering ones kept for refuse.
For one hour was to each of you, or perhaps not
entirely an hour, some span of time that is scarcely
a measure between two whiles, wherein you had
45 existence. Everything. Your veins full of existence.
But we so lightly forget what our laughing neighbor
will neither confirm nor envy. Into the visible
we want to raise it, when even the most visible joy
only can disclose itself to us when we have transformed it
        within.

50 Nowhere, my love, can there be World but within us.
Our life goes by in changing, and ever fainter
dwindles the external. Where an enduring house once stood,
an invented image now strikes across our sight, the concept's
entire property, as though it still loomed in the mind.
55 Vast stores of power the Time Spirit builds itself,
     formless
as that vital drive it levies from all things.
Temples it knows no more. These extravagances of the heart
we are secretly saving. Yes, where there remains
a thing once prayed to, served, or knelt before,
60 it survives, just as it is, into the unseen world.
Many no longer perceive this, still lack the vantage
for building it *inwardly* now, with pillars and statues, greater!

Every dark turn of the world harbors such disinherited ones,
to whom belongs neither the past nor what is to come.
65 For the very nearest thing is distant from mankind. This
should not confuse *us*, but rather reinforce
that preservation in us of the form we still can recognize.
It once *stood* among men, in the face of annihilating Fate,
     stood
in the midst of we-know-not-whither, as if existing, and bowed
70 stars down out of secure heavens. Angel,
to *you* I'll point it out. *There!* in your gaze
it stands at last redeemed, now finally upright.
Pillars, pylons, the Sphinx, cathedral striving to lift
its grey stones out of the crumbling, out of the alien city.

75 Was it no miracle? O marvel, Angel, for *we* are this,
we, O great one. Tell them we did such things; my own
     breath
is too short for the praising of it. So we have not then

entirely neglected our world-space, this generous allotment,
these spaces of *ours*. (And how fearfully great they must be,
80   after these thousands of years still not overcrowded with
          our feelings.)
But a tower was great, was it not? O Angel, it was,—
great even next to you? Chartres was great—and music
reached even higher yet and passed above us. But even
a girl in love, oh, alone at her nightly window . . .
85   didn't she reach to your knee—?
                              Do *not* think I am wooing.
Angel, even if I courted you, you'd not come. For my
call is all the time full of "Away"; against so strong
a current you cannot move. Like an outstretched
90   arm is my calling. And its grasping
upturned open hand remains before you
open, as warning and defense,
Incomprehensible One, wide open.

The Eighth Elegy

With all their eyes all creatures gaze into
the Open. Only our eyes, as though turned in,
on every side of it are set about
like traps to circumvent its free outgoing.
5   What is *without* we know from the face
of animals alone, for even the youngest child
we turn around and force to see the past
as form and not that openness that
lies so deep within the face of animals. Free from death,
10   we alone *see* death; the free animal
has its destruction always behind it
and before it God, so when it moves, it moves
into eternity, like a running spring.
We have never, not for a single day,
15   that pure space before us, into which the flowers
endlessly open: where it is always world
and never Nowhere without No:
that Pure, Unwatched-over, that one breathes and
endlessly *knows* and does not desire. Like a child,
20   one of us will lose himself to it in the stillness

and has to be shaken back. Or another will die and *be* it.
For near to death one perceives death no longer,
and stares *out*, with the animal's wide stare.
Lovers, were not the other there to block
25   the view, come near to it and wonder . . .
How, almost by mistake, it opens up
behind the other . . . though getting past him
is impossible, and world returns again.
Turned always toward creation, we see there
30   only the reflection of that open country
we have obscured. Or how a voiceless beast
will lift his calm glance to look us through and through.
This is our destiny: to be facing
and nothing but that and always facing.

35   Were consciousness after our manner within this
sure beast that draws near to us
but in another direction—, he would pull us with him
on his way. But his being to him is
infinite, incomprehensible and without sight
40   into his situation, pure, like his outward gaze.
And where we see future, he sees all
and himself in all, and is complete forever.

And yet upon this wakeful warm creature
is laid the weight and care of a great sadness.
45   For always there clings to him as well, what often
overwhelms us,—the memory
that what we now press after
once might have been much nearer, truer, and
its attachment infinitely tender. Here all is distance,
50   and there it was breath. After the first homeland
this second is a drafty, hybrid place.

O blessedness of tiny creatures,
who *remain* forever in the womb that bore them;
o joy of the gnat, that can still leap *within*,
55 even on its wedding day: for the womb is everything.
And see the half-assurance of the bird
who from his origin can almost know
of both, like the soul of an Etruscan
come out of a dead man whom that space received
60 for which his resting figure forms the lid.
And how perplexed one is, sprung from the womb
and forced to fly. How frightened of himself.
He rends the air, just as a crack
goes through a china cup. The way the wing
65 of a bat rips through the porcelain of evening.

And we, onlookers, always, everywhere,
turned toward all things and never outward!
It overflows us. We shape it. It decays.
Again we shape it, then decay ourselves.

70 And who has turned us so about that we
whatever we may do, must hold ourselves
like one who is departing? Just as on
the final hill that shows him his whole valley
one last time, a man will turn, and stop, and linger—
75 So we live and forever take our leave.

The Ninth Elegy

Why, when we might spend this span of being,
like the laurel, a little darker than all
the other green, the margin of each leaf fluted
with small waves (like a wind's smile)—: why, then
5   must we be human—and, evading destiny,
long for destiny? . . .

                    Oh *not* because happiness *is,*
that hasty profit of an approaching loss.
Not from curiosity, nor to exercise the heart,
it could have *been* that in the laurel . . . . .

10 But because being present is so much, because it seems
that what is here is in need of us, this fading world
has strangely charged us. Us who fade the most. *Once*
to everything, only *once. Once* and no more. And we too,
once. And never again. But this
15 *once* to have been, if only this *once:*
to have been of the earth seems beyond revoking.

And so we press on and attempt to achieve it,
wanting to contain it in our simple hands,
in the overcrowded gaze and in the speechless heart.
20 We try to become it. To give it to whom? Much rather
would we keep it forever . . . But, in that other relation
alas, what can we bring there? Not that perception we've
learned here so slowly, and nothing that has happened here.
Nothing. And so, the pain. And above all the heaviness,
25 the long experience of love, the truly unspeakable things.
But later, under the stars, what then: *they* are *better* left
       untold.
For the wanderer brings down from the mountainside
not a handful of earth to the valley, all indescribable,
but the word he has gained there, pure, the yellow
30 and blue gentian. Are we perhaps here only to say: house,
bridge, brook, gate, jug, olive tree, window,—
at best: pillar, tower . . . but to *say* them, understand me,
so to say them as the things within themselves never
thought to be. Is not the hidden craft
35 of this secretive earth when she urges two lovers on,
that in their feelings each and every thing should be
       transported?
Threshold: what is it for two
lovers that they wear down a little
the older threshold of their own door. They too, after
40 the many before them, and before all those to come . . . ,
       lightly.

Here is the time for what can be *told*, here its home.
Speak and confess. More than ever
do the things we live with fall away, and
what displaces them is an act without image.
45 An act under crusts it will rip as soon

as its strength outgrows them and seeks new limits.
Between the hammer strokes
our heart endures, as does
the tongue between the teeth, which still
50 is able to praise.

Praise to the Angel our world, not the untellable:
you can't impress *him* with grand emotion. In the cosmos
where he so powerfully feels, you're only a newcomer.
Then show him some simple thing, grown up through
       generations
55 till it became ours, and lives near our hands and in our eyes.
Tell him of things and he'll stand astonished, as you stood
beside the rope-maker in Rome, or with the Nile potter.
Show him how joyful a thing can be, how innocent and ours,
how even lamenting sorrow can take purely its own form,
60 serve as a thing, or die in a thing—and in ecstasy
escape beyond the violin. And these things,
that live only in passing, understand that you praise them;
fugitive, they look to us, the most fugitive, for rescue.
They want us entirely to transform them in our invisible
       hearts
65 into—oh, infinitely—into us! Whoever we finally are.

Earth, is not this what you want: *invisibly*
to arise in us? Is it not your dream
to become one day invisible?—Earth! invisible!
What do you charge us with if not transformation?
70 Earth, my love, I will. Oh believe me, I need
no more of your springtimes to win me; *one*,
ah just one is already too much for my blood.
Unutterably I am resolved to be yours, from afar.

75 You were always right, and your holiest occurrence
    is our intimate companion, Death.

    Look, I live. And for what? Neither childhood nor future
    grows any less in me . . . . . Unaccountable being
    springs up in my heart.

The Tenth Elegy

That I one day, with the passing of this grim vision,
might sing out jubilant praise to assenting Angels.
That from the clear-struck keys of my heart, not one
should fail from doubtful, or slack or breaking strings;
5   that my streaming face might make me more radiant,
until an inconspicuous weeping bloom there. How dear
will you be to me then, you nights of sorrowing.
Oh why did I not, disconsolate sisters, kneel
more to receive you, give myself more loosely
10   into your loosened hair. We, wasting our sorrows,
how we gaze beyond them into some drab duration
to see if they may not end there. While already
they are the winter foliage, our darkened evergreen,
one of the seasons of our secret year—, not only
15   season—, but place, settlement, camp, soil, habitation.

Ah, but really, how strange are the streets of the city of grief,
where, in the false stillness of an overreaching clamor,
strong from the spout of a casting of emptiness,
swaggers that gilded confusion, the collapsing monument.

20 How an Angel would crush beyond trace their market of
        comfort,
    with its church alongside, bought ready-made:
    clean and shut and disillusioned as a post office on Sunday.
    But outside there is always the curling rim of the fair,
    swings of freedom! High-divers and jugglers of enthusiasm!
25 And the lifelike ranges of dressed-up chance
    where the targets teeter off the rack with a tinny sound
    when a crack shot steps up. From applause to new conquests
    he goes reeling on, for booths that can tempt all the curious
    are barking and drumming. But for adults
30 there is something special to see: how money breeds itself,
    anatomically, not only for amusement: all its golden genitals,
    the whole works, the facts—, both educational and to increase
    fertility. . . . .
                            . . . Oh but just outside,
35 behind the last billboard, plastered with placards of
        "Deathless,"
    that bitter beer that seems so sweet to its drinkers
    as long as they chew on plenty of fresh distractions . . . ,
    just in back of those planks, just behind, is the *real* world
    where children play, and lovers hold each other,—to the side,
40 gravely, in the sparse grass, where the dogs follow nature.
    The young man walks farther on; perhaps loving a youthful
    lament . . . He escorts her onto the meadows. She says:
    —It's pretty far. We live way out there. . . .
                            Where? And the young man
45 follows. He's moved by her bearing. Her shoulders,
        her neck—,
    perhaps she comes of a noble line. But he leaves her,
        turns back,
    looks around, waves . . . What is the use? She is a lament.

Only the young dead, in their earliest state
of timeless serenity, while being weaned away,
50 follow her lovingly. Girls
she awaits and befriends, shows them gently
what she wears. Pearls of grief and the fine-spun
veils of enduring. Young men she will walk beside
silently.

55 But there where they dwell in the valley, one of the older
laments attends to the youth when he questions her:—
    We were once,
she says, a great clan, we laments. Our fathers
drove their mines deep in that mountain range. Among men
you sometimes find a polished bit of ancient sorrow,
60 or from the slag of an old volcano, some petrified rage.
Yes, that came from here too. Once we were rich.—

And lightly she leads him through the far-flung land of
        lamentation,
shows him the temple columns or the ruins
of those strongholds where the lords of lament once ruled
65 the land wisely. Shows him the tall
trees of tears and fields of flowering sadness,
(the living know them only as tender leaves);
shows him the pasturing herds of grief,—and sometimes
a bird takes fright and wings low across their gaze,
70 inscribing the distant lettered image of its desolate cry.—
At evening she leads him on to the graves of the elders
of the house of lament, the sybils and seers of warning.
With night coming on, they wander more slowly and soon
there moons up above, the tomb
75 overwatching all, twin brother to that on the Nile,
the sublime Sphynx, countenance of the secret chamber.

And they marvel at the regal head that silently
has laid the human face
forever on the scale of the stars.

80   His sight cannot quite grasp it, from early death
still dizzy. But her glance
frightens an owl from the rim of the crown. And the bird,
brushing a slow stroke along the cheek—
the one with ripest rounding—
85   faintly inscribes on the new hearing
of the dead, as on a double cut-open page,
the indescribable outline.

And above it the stars, the new ones. The stars of grief's
        country.
Slowly she names them: "Here,
90   look: the *Rider*, the *Staff*, and that fuller constellation
they call *Fruit-garland*. Then on toward the pole:
Cradle; Way; the Burning Book; Doll; Window.
But in the southern sky, pure as the palm
of a blessed hand, the clear gleaming "M",
95   that stands for Mothers. . . . .—

But the dead must continue, and silently the older
lament brings him to the rim of the gorge
where it shines in the moonlight,
the fount of joy. In reverence
100   she names it, saying:—Among men
it is a bearing stream.—

They stand at the foot of the mountains.
And there she embraces him weeping.

Alone he climbs into the mountains of primal grief.
105 And not once does his step ring from this soundless fate.

Yet within us the endless dead were waking a likeness;
see, they were pointing perhaps to the catkins hung
from the empty hazels, or suggesting the rain
that falls on the dark soil in early spring.—

110 And we, who have always counted
on joy as *ascending*, would suffer
the emotion that almost alarms us
when a joyful thing falls.

APPENDIX

FIVE ADDITIONAL POEMS
TRANSLATED BY STEPHEN GARMEY

APPENDIX

Anti-strophes

(ORIGINALLY THE FIFTH ELEGY)

Oh, that you should be here, women, walking
along among us, full of sorrow and
no more sheltered than we, and for all that
able to make blissful like the Blessed.

5 From where,
when the beloved appears,
will you take the future?
More than ever there will be.
He who knows the distance
10 to the farthest fixed star
marvels when he must concede it
to your own great heart-space.
How in the pressing crowd do you leave it open?
You, full of springs and full of night.

15 Was it really you
when you were children,
and surly in the school yard
when your older brother pushed you?
You sound ones.

Lines 1–4: Venice, summer 1912; lines 5–49: Muzot, February 9, 1922.

20 When we as children already were
    twisting ourselves ugly for ever,
    you were like bread for the consecration.

    The breaking off of childhood
    brought you no harm. At once
25 you stood there as if suddenly
    restored to wonder in God.

    We, as though broken from some mountain,
    even as boys with sharp edges,
    perhaps often auspiciously hewn,
30 we fell like stone chips
    over flowers.

    Flowers in the deeper soil
    and loved by every root,
    you, the sisters of Euridice
35 forever full of holy return
    behind the climbing man.

    We, having offended ourselves,
    gladly offending and again gladly
    by necessity offended.
40 We, our anger
    laid like weapons near our sleep.

    You, almost like protection in the place
    where no one protects. Like a shady tree of sleep
    is the thought of you
45 for the throngs of the lonely one.

    [We, in the struggling nights,
    we fall from nearness to nearness;
    and where the beloved melts,
    we are a plunging stone.]

Original Version
of the Tenth Elegy

O that someday, with the passing of this grim vision,
I might sing out jubilant praise to assenting angels;
that of all the clear-struck keys of my heart, none
should fail on doubtful, slack or irrascible strings;
5   that my streaming face might make me more radiant,
with an inconspicuous weeping bloom there. How dear
will you be to me then, you nights of sorrowing.
Oh why did I not, disconsolate sisters, kneel
more to receive you, give myself more loosely
10   into your loosened hair. We, spendthrifts of sorrows.
How we gaze beyond them into some drab duration
to see if they may not end there. But they are
seasons of ourselves, our winter-
worn foliage, meadows, ponds, our inborn landscape
15   inhabited by sedge creatures and birds.

High overhead does not the half of heaven
hang above our melancholy, our belabored nature?
Think, if you trod no more the weed-grown state of your grief,
saw no more the stars through the harsher rustling

Begun at Duino in 1912; completed in Paris at the end of 1913.

20 of swarthy pain-leaves; if aggrandizing moonlight
    no more exalted for you the ruins of fate,
    to let you feel yourself through them some former race?
    Smiling too, would be no more, the consuming smile of those
    you lose beyond,—with so little violence
25 and passing you, they came pure into your pain.
    (Almost like the girl who gives her suitor
    who for weeks has pressed her, her promise, and
    straightway brings him startled to the garden gate, that
              triumphant
    man so reluctant to leave: then a step in this more recent
              parting
30 troubles her, she waits and stands, and her entire glancing up
    now strikes the stranger's upglance, glancing up of the virgin
    who grasps him endlessly, the outsider intended for her,
    outside wandering other, eternally intended for her.
    Echoing, he passes on.) Such was constantly your losing;
35 never the possessor: but as one who is dying,
    bent forward into the wet blowing March night,
    oh, loses the spring down the throats of the birds.

    Far too much do you belong in suffering. Should you forget
    the least of its immeasurably grieved forms,
40 you would call down, cry down, hoping for earlier
              inquisitiveness,
    one of the angels, incapable of pain, forever attempting
    with darkened, difficult expression to describe for you
    the sobbing for it you once made.
    Angel, what was it like? And he would imitate you,
45 not understand that it was grief; as one will
    imitate the guiltless voice that filled a crying bird.

Exposed upon the mountains of the heart. Look, how
    small there!
look: the last village of words, and higher,
but again how small, still one last
homestead of feeling. Can you make it out?
5 Exposed upon the mountains of the heart. Stone ground
under your hands. Though some things
bloom here well enough; singing out from the
mute precipice blooms an unknowing plant.
But the one who does know? Ah, began to know
10 and now keeps silence, exposed upon the mountains of
    the heart.
Here there wanders with undamaged cognizance
still some life, some safe mountain beast
passes and lingers. And the great protected bird
is circling round the pure refusal of the summit.—But
unprotected, here upon the mountains of the heart. . . .

Munich, September 20, 1914.

The Death of Moses

Not one, except the dark and fallen angel
would respond, take weapons, undertake the death
of him who had been summoned. Then even he
came clattering backward, upward
5   screaming into heaven: No. I cannot!

For through the thicket of his brows
coolly Moses had noticed him and gone on writing:
words of blessing and the everlasting Name.
And his eye was clear right to the ground of his strength.

10   Therefore the Lord himself, dragging half of heaven
        with him,
forced his way down, made up a bed of the very mountain;
laid out the old man. From its well-ordered dwelling
he summoned the soul; up!, and there to recount
the many things they had in common, their uncountable
        friendship.

15   But for the soul at last it was enough. The completed one
conceded that it was enough. Then slowly to the aged man

Lines 1–14: Paris, summer 1914; lines 15–21: Munich, October 1915.

82

the aged God bowed down his aged face. In his kiss
received him from himself into his older age. And with
      creating hands
closed again the mountain; so that now, refashioned,
20   it should be but one among the mountains of the earth,
unrecognizable to men.

Elegy on Childhood

That once there was childhood, let that nameless
loyalty of heaven, let it not be withdrawn by Fate.
Even the prisoner, perishing dark in his jail
has it looked after right to the end, with its old
5   timeless hold on the heart. And even the afflicted man
staring and understanding, when already his
room will no longer respond, being curable—, curable
like everything lying around; just as feverish, sick
but yet curable—; even for *him*
10   childhood bears fruit. Cleanly
amid decaying nature it keeps its friendly garden.
Not that it is harmless; the prettifying error
that aprons and frills it does not long deceive.
It is no more safe than we, and never more protected;
15   nothing god-like counterbalances its weight; as defenceless
as we are; as beasts in winter are defenceless.
More defenceless still: for it knows of no hiding place.
     Defenceless
as though it were itself what threatened. Defenceless
as a flame, as a giant, as poison, as what goes around
20   at night in the suspicious house with bolted doors.

    Berg am Irschel, 1921.

For who has not yet grasped that the protecting hands
tell lies; defending—they are themselves in danger: who *may*
    then?
"I!"—Which I?—"I, your mother, I may. I was fore-world.
To me has the earth confided what she works in the seed
25 to keep it sound. Evenings, oh, of confiding, when softly and
    springlike
we rained ourselves, Earth and I, into the womb.
Masculine! Oh who will demonstrate to *you* the pregnant
harmony we felt together. For *you* the silence of the universe
announces nothing, closes itself around no growing thing . . ."

30 A mother's magnanimity, the voice of quieting, and yet!
What you name, it *is* the danger, the whole pure
peril of the world—, and thus it turns,
as it is moving you, into defence. Fervent childhood
stands within it as a center, *out*-fearing it and fearless.

35 But fear! Is learned all at once in that transaction
fashioned by our leaking humanity. Draftily
it pokes in through the cracks. There it is. From behind
it scurries in over the play, the child, and hisses
seeds of discord into his blood—, the quick suspicions that
40 only part will later on be grasped, always
some one piece of existence, some five, but all never capable
of being joined together, all brittle. And in the spine
already the twig of a will would split,
fork into a doubting branch growing hard
45 on the Judas-tree of choice.
How it bribes the good-natured doll, that just now
most tender of playthings, gives it strange chill even
there in the child's arms—. But not with itself, not with its
    own poor

pardonable strangeness, no: with the child's disposition,
     with what
50 he has received. Received on long days of confiding, in those
     countless
hours of confessing play, when he lifted and proved
     himself
against the unenvying, distantly fashioning You—
came, by dividing his strength with another, to experience
     himself
and his own so freshly growing reserves.

55 Expanses of playing! Then the ripening self passed further on
in more blissful discovery, in the latest generation
far beyond grandchildren—, that trusting nature!
Friend of death, for in easy transformation
it grew through death a hundred times . . . O doll, remote
     figure—,
60 as stars practice by standing apart to be worlds
you make the child into a star.
Is cosmic space for a child too small: space for the feelings
you stretch in amazement between you, intensified space.

But all of a sudden it happens . . . What? When? That
     nameless disruption—
65 What? the Betrayal . . . Filled with the half of existence
the doll wants no more, disowns, refuses to recognize.
Stares with unwilling eyes, lies down, doesn't know; not even
a thing any more—look how the things
are ashamed for it,

. . . .

COMMENTARY

Lines 1–2: . . . *the order*
of Angels . . .

At the time the First Elegy was written Rilke associated angels with the superhuman powers of art: the voices he felt were summoning him to his real task, and away from the merely human life in which he considered himself a failure. He described that task as a recording of the world "seen no more with human eyes but in the angel."[1] He had written to Baron Uexküll in 1909:

To regard art not as a selection from the world but as a radical transformation of the world into the glorious. The wonderment with which art flings itself on things (all things, without exception), must be so impetuous, so strong, so radiant, that the thing has no time to remember its own ugliness or depravity. In the sphere of the terrible there can be nothing so canceling or negative that the effect on it of artistic accomplishment would not leave it with a great, positive excess, like something that now asserts life, wills it to be: like an angel.[2]

1. *B. aus M.*, 80 (dated October 27, 1915).
2. *B. 1907–1914*, 74 (dated August 19, 1909).

But the angels themselves struck terror in Rilke.

Lines 4–7:   . . . *For beauty is only*
the beginning of terror we can just barely endure,
and what we so admire is its calm
disdaining to destroy us. . . .

A letter Rilke wrote at about the same time as the First Elegy
throws light on this passage:

for the powers . . . are not altogether destructive though they
occasionally lead to ruin; that is only the reverse side of any great
power: what the Old Testament means by saying that you can't
really begin to see an angel and not die from the exposure.[3]

But terrifying as Rilke's voices were to him, he was resolved
to strain his ear to hear them and forego such help with the
human side of his life as psychoanalysis offered, for fear he
would lose them in the process: lose his ability to be an artist.

By the time the Seventh Elegy was written (1922) the
meaning angels held for Rilke had been augmented. The
famous statement of that final meaning occurs in his letter of
November 13, 1925 to Witold von Hulewicz, his Polish
translator. But as it refers more precisely to the angel of the
later elegies, it is perhaps premature to read it back more
than thirteen years into the first two. (See notes on lines 83–
84, p. 91; on lines 49 and 70 of the Seventh Elegy, pp. 102
and 103; and on lines 62–63 of the Tenth Elegy, p. 105.)

Line 10:   . . . *Neither Angels nor men,*

it goes badly with me when I wait for human beings, need human
beings, look around for human beings.[4]

3. *Ibid.*, 196 (dated February 11, 1912).
4. *Ibid.*, 149 (dated December 28, 1911).

angels are too passionate to be good observers. They excell us in action no less than God excells them; I regard them as assailants *par excellence,*—and here you must give in to me: I can vouch for it. For having come painstakingly from things and from animals, I then longed to be instructed in humanity; but behold, the Angelic was imparted to me, and therefore I have skipped over people.[5]

Line 11: *the ingenious beasts*

The German word translated "ingenious" is *findigen* meaning literally, "path-finding."

Lines 29–30: . . . *a violin*
              gave itself up. . . .

Strange violin, are you following me? In how many cities has your lonely night already spoken to mine? Are hundreds of people playing you? Or only one? Are there, in all great cities, those who, without you, would already have lost themselves in the rivers? And why does it always affect me the way it does? Why am I always the neighbor of those who anxiously compel you to sing and to say: Life is more difficult than the difficulty of everything else?[6]

Line 30: . . . *All this was a charge.*

The word Rilke used for "charge" is *Auftrag,* meaning literally, to "bear up" or "carry up." The critic, Geoffrey H. Hartman writes:

[Rilke's] words aim to render the physical rather than the historical, social, emotional, or religious connotations. Rilke attempts to create a new idiom which would neglect the anthropomorphic for the physical basis of language. The commonplace sense of words is neglected for their seeming origin as signs signifying weight, direction, and invisibly oriented gesture. Rilke's poetry is made difficult for the foreign reader by the amount of etymological play that restores compound words (*aufstehen, angehen, entragen*) to

5. *Ibid.,* 275 (dated March 15, 1913).
6. "Der Nachbar," *G.W.,* ii, 42.

the meaning held by the sum of their individual components. This does not mean that ordinary connotations are always neglected or are out of harmony: the word *Auftrag,* used at two significant points in the *Elegies* . . . shows a happy coincidence of common-place and physical meanings.[7]

Line 46: . . . *Gaspara Stampa* . . .

An Italian girl, born in 1523, who was deserted by her lover, the Count Collatine di Collato, and died at the age of thirty-one. In her grief, she wrote a series of two hundred sonnets, and consoled herself with other lovers and religion. Rilke wrote to a friend on January 23, 1912:

what speaks to me immensely of humanity, and with an authori-tative calm that makes my hearing full of room, is the vision of those who have died young, and even more unconditionally still, more purely, more inexhaustibly: the woman who loves.[8]

Lines 50–51:   . . . *Is it not time that our loving*
                      freed us from our beloved and we, trembling,
                      endured;

Rilke was impressed by Marianne Alcoforado, a Portuguese nun, who once wrote to a man in love with her:

"My love depends no longer on the way you treat me." . . . she does not fling the stream of her feelings into the imaginary, but rather with unending strength leads the ingenuity of these feelings back into herself: enduring it, nothing else.[9]

Line 65:   *as recently the tablet in Santa Maria Formosa?*

Rilke had visited this church in Venice in 1911. Romano Guardini suggests that a plaque near the right side-altar may be the one which Rilke remembered. Its inscription reads:

---

7. *The Unmediated Vision,* 95.
8. *B. 1907–1914,* 176.
9. *Ibid.,* 178.

"For others I lived, as long as life lasted. Yet finally, after I have died, I have not been extinguished, but in cold marble I live for myself. I was Hermann Wilhelm. Flanders mourns me. Adria sighs for me, poverty calls me. He died September 16, 1593."[10]

Lines 83–84: . . . *The eternal torrent*
hurls all ages along through both realms

Affirmation of life—AND—death turns out to be one thing in the Elegies. Here it is learned and celebrated that to grant the one without the other would ultimately exclude everything infinite. Death is the side of life turned away from us, the side we do not illuminate: we must try to reach the greatest awareness of our existence which is at home in both these unlimited realms, inexhaustibly nurtured by both. . . . The true contours of life extend through both regions; the blood with the greatest circulation flows through both: there is neither a this-world nor an otherworld, but the great unity in which the beings which surpass us, the "Angels," are at home.[11]

Line 91: . . . *in mourning for Linos*

Linos was originally a god of Greek nature-worship. The Linos song (*Iliad* 18.570) is a dirge for the end of summer. Linos was loved for his beauty, and when he died those who had known him were stricken with "rigid bleakness." The void he left behind was itself startled by the loss, and its vibrant amazement was called music.

SECOND ELEGY

Line 3: . . . *the days of Tobias* . . .

Tobias was an Israelite whose story is told in the Apocryphal Book of *Tobit*. He was sent by Tobit, his father, a prisoner

10. *Rilkes Deutung des Daseins*, 61–62.
11. *B. aus M.*, 332–333 (dated November 13, 1925).

of Ninevah, to retrieve some sacks of silver being held for him at Rhages in Media. Tobias did not know the way to Rhages, so at his father's suggestion he "went out to look for a man who knew the way" and "found Raphael the angel standing facing him though he did not guess he was an angel of God." He asked him, "Do you know the road to Media?" and Raphael replied, "Certainly I do, I have been there many times." So "the boy left with the angel and the dog followed behind."[12]

Lines 16–17:   mirrors: *each drawing back into its counte-*
                        nance again
                   its own outstreamed beauty.

Rilke wrote about the Portuguese nun, Marianna Alcoforado:

had it pleased God to try with her what he constantly does with the angels, when he casts their whole radiance back into them—: I am sure, on the spot, as she stood there in that sad convent, she would have become an angel, within, in her deepest nature.[13]

Line 57:   . . . *the place you tender ones have covered*

Rilke commented on an Italian translation of the Second Elegy which Princess Marie made in 1913:

I am apprehensive about the phrase so dear to me, concerning the lovers. . . . This is meant quite literally, that the place where the lover lays his hand is thereby witheld from passing away, from aging, from all that near-decay that is always happening in our essential selves—it simply *lasts, is,* under his hand. It must be possible, just as literally, to make this clear in Italian; it is simply lost in any paraphrase.[14]

Line 72:   . . . *only so to touch each other* . . .

I believe that once in Naples, standing in front of some ancient gravestone, it flashed through me that I should never touch people

12. *Tobit,* 5; 4–6 (Jerusalem Bible, London, D.L.T., 610-611).
13. *B. 1907–1914,* 178 (dated January 23, 1912).
14. *RMR-MTT,* i, 334–335 (dated December 16, 1913).

with stronger gestures than those depicted there. And I really believe sometimes that I have come far enough along to express all the rushing of my heart, without loss or undoing, when I lay my hand lightly on a shoulder. Wouldn't that, Lou, wouldn't that be the single improvement thinkable within that "restraint" you remind me of?[15]

THIRD ELEGY

Line 21: . . . *your offending touch* . . . .

The German is *beruhrenden Anstoss*, which literally means that the offence, *Anstoss*, is doing the touching.

Line 30: *you stood between him and this surging chaos*

The German is *vertratst* which brings an ambivalence into play, in that it can mean either "stand in the way of" or "block," as well as "represent as an advocate."

Line 82: . . . *some reliable task* . . .

Rilke often referred in the first few weeks of 1912 to an experience he once had at Capri:

I would sit with two old women and a young girl and watch their handiwork, and sometimes at the end I was given an apple one of them had peeled. . . . I experienced there something almost like the mystical nourishment of the sacrament.[16]

what I would give to see sometimes in the evening a woman's two hands active with some manual task, almost spiritually—not to mention that now there is no one here even to peel an apple for me. From that sight, that act of kindness I drew strength for years to come.[17]

I have never looked more ardently than in the last year, on those who can manage some good, regular task which they can always

15. *RMR-LAS*, 256 (dated January 10, 1912).
16. *Ibid.*, 254.
17. *B. 1907–1914*, 154 (dated January 2, 1912).

do, something which depends more on intellect, thought, under-
standing, skill—how do I know—than on these violent, interior
tensions over which one has no control.[18]

On March 2, 1912, Rilke gave Princess Marie one further ex-
ample of what the "reliable task" meant to him:

it is enough to see the gardner bending down somewhere, to begin
to feel moved, almost as though the simple, industrious tasks he
does there, had to be, and had value for oneself as well—as
though in oneself, too, things must be put in their right place, en-
couraged and bound up. . . .[19]

FOURTH ELEGY

Line 1:   *O trees of life, when does your winter come?*

In his September 6, 1915 letter to Princess Marie, Rilke wrote:

autumn has so suddenly overtaken us, here at last. I look out from
unfamiliar windows at the tree-lined embankment of the Isar,
yellowing; and under the cold rain the yellows are not waiting
their turn, but the next-to-last shades are already there and soon
the leaves will begin falling. These rainy nights and winter at the
door—and the widespread misery pools together with my own,
with my helplessness in the face of tomorrow. . . . All my knowl-
edge is confined to the very negative realization that I should not
stay in Munich any longer. The people here make too many
claims on you; you have to be *completed* or feign that you are,—
*et moi, si j'ai encore quelque avenir, ce sera en recommençant
humblement que j'y parviendrai,* for anything in my books that
might be counted (to a certain extent) completed, that too is over
and done for me. . . . I stand here like a beginner, though of
course like one who is not beginning anything.[20]

18. *Ibid.*, 165–166 (dated January 12, 1912).
19. *RMR-MTT*, i, 120.
20. *RMR-MTT*, i, 437–438.

Years later, he wrote to a friend:

Almost all the war years, *par hasard plutôt*, I was waiting in Munich, always believing that it must come to an end, not realizing, not realizing, not being able to realize. . . .[21]

Lines 19, 21–22; *Who has not sat before the curtain of his heart, frightened?*

· · ·

. . . The familiar garden, and swaying slightly . . .

The imagery here was perhaps influenced by a short sketch which Rilke wrote in 1899, *Frau Blaha's Magd*.[22] In it, a half-wit girl, Annushka, is hired as a maid; she is raped but doesn't realize what the outcome will be until one morning she gives birth in the attic. She strangles the screaming child with the blue ribbons of her apron, and later wraps the tiny corpse in a trunk. She then invests her savings in a puppet theatre

whose curtain goes up and down making the garden on the backdrop take turns appearing and disappearing. Now Annushka had something to make up for her loneliness. . . . But often when she had just rolled up the curtain, she would run quickly to the front of the stage and stare into the garden, and the whole gray kitchen would vanish behind the tall, magnificent trees.[23]

She promises the neighborhood children who come to watch the puppet show the biggest doll they have ever seen, the "big, blue one," but before she has time to get it, they all leave. She then wildly tramples down the stage in the dark kitchen and smashes the heads of all the puppets, including the "big, blue one."

21. *B. 1914–1921* (dated January 21, 1920).
22. *S.W.*, iv, 623.
23. *Ibid.*, 628–629.

Lines 23–25:   *Not* him. *Enough. However gracefully he move*
         he is disguised, and turns into a tradesman who goes into his house through the kitchen door.

This dancer is not the one the audience expected, in fact he is not a real dancer, but only a disguised tradesman so eager to get home for dinner that he uses the kitchen door to his house.

Lines 27–28:   *but rather, the doll.* . . .
         the wire and the rags for dress.

Rilke is referring here to marionettes as representing art almost come to life. But the word *puppe* also means doll in German and conveys Rilke's

> dual attitude toward art, a deep-seated discord, never quite resolved. . . . For although art, or the puppet, seemed preferable by far to life, nevertheless its disillusioning nature, its apparent impotence to act on life was also represented. The puppet created by man stood, not for absolute art, but for human approximation to it, and in particular Rilke's own poetry, whose inadequacy in the face of the war was the saddest lesson he ever learned. Hence his insistence that the puppet was filled with sawdust, that its face was completely inexpressive, and the wires all too visible. Having dismissed his fellow human beings from his life, this was what he was faced with, and he had to do so in utter isolation from his own kind.[24]

Rilke described the associations dolls had for him in a short piece he wrote in 1914:

> If we were . . . to find one of these dolls—pulling it out from under a pile of friendlier things, it would almost irk us with its frightful, thick forgetfulness; the enmity which no doubt has always been an unconscious part of our relationship, would rear up and expose itself before us as the foreign body on which we

24. E. M. Butler, *Rilke*, 331.

had squandered our purest warmth—as the thinly painted drowned body which had let itself be lifted and carried on our flooding tenderness until the tide went out and it was forgotten somewhere in the tangled weeds. I know, I know we had to have such things which always agreed with us in everything. The simplest exchanges of love were way beyond us, we couldn't possibly have lived with anyone who *was* something, or had any dealings with him. . . .[25]

Line 35: . . . *the boy with the brown bent eye*

The reference is to Rilke's cousin, Egon von Rilke, who died at an early age and with whom Rilke had played as a child. Carl Sieber writes that he once said:

I think of him often and am always coming back to the image of him which has remained indescribably moving to me. So much "childhood," the brokenhearted and helpless side of childhood, is embodied for me in his form, in the ruff he wore, in his little neck, in his chin, in his beautiful brown eyes disfigured by a squint.[26]

Line 37: *Am I not right? Father,* . . .

J. R. von Salis recalls that Rilke often said in conversation that his father had tried to do what was best for him. But Rilke wrote at the end of January 1914:

when I think of my father, I am almost sure now that . . . he was not able to love; in his heart he had until he died a kind of inexpressible anxiety toward me, an emotion against which I was almost defenceless, which may have cost him more than the most tremendous love. . . .[27]

And in the autobiographical story, *Ewald Tragy:*

my father, he is an excellent man, I love him. He is so elegant, and his heart is pure gold. But people ask him: "What is your son?" And he is ashamed and gets embarrassed. What should he say?

25. *Some Reflections on Dolls, G.W.,* iv, 268–269.
26. *René Rilke,* 59–60.
27. Magda von Hattingberg, *Rilke und Benvenuta,* 21–22.

Only a poet? That's simply absurd. Even if it were possible—it's no profession. It provides no income, one would have no rank or class, be eligible for no pension, in short, have no real connection with life. Therefore one should not endorse this kind of thing, certainly not give it one's approval. Now do you realize why I never show my father anything I have done, or, as a rule anyone else around here, because they don't judge my efforts, they hate me in them. And I myself have so much doubt. You know—I lay awake all night wringing my hands and wondering whether I have any worth at all.[28]

Line 56:   . . . *rags.*

The German word, *Balg,* literally means "skin," or a puppet's body, or in slang, "brat" or "urchin."

Line 73:   *in the between-spaces between the world and*
          our toys

In his essay on dolls, Rilke evoked the spirit of a rocking horse:

Great, gallant soul of the rocking horse, you are the rocking waves of a boy's heart, you churned up the play-room air until it did handsprings like the air over one of the world's famous battlefields: proud, trustworthy, almost visible soul. How you made the walls and window cross-bars, the daily horizons, rattle as though these most temporary arrangements, which on stand-still afternoons could seem so invincible, were already being assaulted by the storms of the future.[29]

Line 76:   *Who will present a child just as he stands? . . .*

In the second of his essays on Rodin, Rilke wrote about a child's relationship with *things:*

If it is possible, return with at least a part of your feelings, removed from the scene and grown-up as they are, to any one of the child-

28. *S.W.,* iv, 512.
29. *G.W.,* iv, 273–274.

hood things that used to keep you company. And just think, did anything ever get closer to you, more intimate, more necessary to you? Was not everything else *except* it, not beyond causing you pain or being unfair, frightening you with heartache or entangling you with uncertainty? If there was kindliness among your first experiences, or confidence, or the feeling that you were not alone, was that not thanks to *it?* Was it not with such a thing that you first shared your little heart as if it were a piece of bread that served for two?

Later on, didn't you find in the legends of the saints a quiet joyousness, a humility which had been blessed, a willingness to be all things—qualities which you were already acquainted with because some small piece of wood had once accomplished them all for you, undertaken and borne them for you. That small, forgotten object that was prepared to be everything for you, gave you confidence in a thousand things by playing for you a thousand parts, whether it were animal or tree or king or child; and when that was done and it stepped back, all these were there. That same thing, worthless as it was, had prepared your first connections with the world, had let you into what was happening and into relationship with people. And more than that: in its presence, its being, its appearance whatever that was, and when it finally broke to pieces or slipped away mysteriously, you had met with everything human, had even gone deep into death itself.[30]

Lines 79–81:   . . . *leave it*
                there within his round mouth like the core
                of an enticing apple? . . .

An adult immediately removes the core from his mouth when he has eaten an apple. Not so, a child: he likes to keep it there, and someone has to come and take it out before it chokes him. Rilke is saying that a child does not mind death any more than he minds an apple's core in his mouth which could choke him. Only adults reject either a core or death.

30. *Ibid.,* 377–378.

FIFTH ELEGY

Line 10:   *lost in space,* . . .

Art without love, symbolized by the acrobats' tricks which for
all their virtuosity are done "in jest," was now as meaningless
to Rilke as a "tin plate" rolled down a table (lines 17–18),
it had for him no real place in the world.

Lines 14–15:   . . . *like the large initials*
                 of Standing-there . . .

Romano Guardini writes:

Someone who knew Rilke very well for a long time gave me an
interpretation [of this] which is both simple and profound. This
is an example of a form of expression which Rilke is supposed to
have been very fond of. If, for example—here I am reproducing
exactly what was told to me—Rilke saw a beautiful woman, he
might have said "she is the initial letter of beauty."[31]

Line 17:   . . . *August the Strong*

King of Poland and Elector of Saxony, 1670–1733, who pre-
sided over a dissolute and extravagant court.

Lines 37–38, 41:   *O you*
                     that during one drawn-out recovery
                                    . . .
                     You that . . .

These characters in the poem remain obscure. Rilke admitted
to Marga Wertheimer:

You may be right, perhaps the experience behind the poem should
be more clearly indicated, since the poet himself is the one most
likely to overlook such necessities.[32]

31. *Rilke's Duino Elegies,* 136.
32. Marga Wertheimer, *Arbeitsstunden mit R.M.R.,* 43–44, cited by
Heerikhuizen, *op. cit.,* 327–328.

Lines 63: *"Subrisio Saltat."*

Abbreviated from *subrisio saltatoris*, acrobat's smile.

Line 90: . . . *the modiste,* Madame Lamort

When Rilke first went to Paris he was struck by all the different degrees of death he saw. In a letter to Lou Andreas-Salome, he wrote:

I went past long hospitals, whose doors stand open with a gesture of impatient and craving charity . . . saw people . . . for whom affliction had fashioned special organs, organs of hunger and death. They bore the bleak, discolored mimicry of those overgrown cities, and endured *life* under the foot of each day as it stepped on them like wiry beetles. . . .[33]

SIXTH ELEGY

Line 8: *See: like the God into the swan.*

Jupiter, who had transformed himself into a swan, raped Leda before he had even had a chance to enjoy his new shape, take pride in his blooming (line 10).

Line 20: . . . *Karnak* . . .

In January 1911, Rilke visited Karnak and described it in a letter to his wife:

that mysterious temple-world of Karnak which I saw . . . yesterday under a moon only just beginning to wane. Saw, saw, saw—my God, you pull yourself together, try with all your will to believe your two focused eyes; and yet it begins above them—reaches in all directions beyond them (only a god can cultivate such a field of vision)—a calyx column stands there like a lone survivor, and you don't encompass it, because it stands far out beyond our life; only together with the night somehow, can you comprehend it,

33. *RMR-LAS,* 55 (dated July 18, 1903).

take it in along with the stars, when for a second it becomes human—human experience.[34]

SEVENTH ELEGY

Line 36:   *Do not believe Fate to be more than the wisdom of childhood;*

In his *Letters to a Young Poet* Rilke wrote:

that which we call fate does not come to us from the outside; it comes out from within us. But because so many people have not absorbed their destinies while they lived in them and have not transformed them within themselves, they have not recognized what has gone out from them. It was so strange to them that, in their confused panic, they thought it must have just then entered them and they swear they have never found anything like it in themselves before.[35]

Line 49:   . . . *when we have transformed it within.*

Transformed? Yes, for it is our task to imprint this interim, perishable world earth so deeply in ourselves, so tolerantly, so passionately that its essence will arise in us again "invisibly." . . . The *Elegies* show us at this work, the work of these continuing transformations of the beloved visible and tangible world into the invisible vibrations and stimulation of our nature.[36]

Line 53:   *schlagt . . . vor* commonly means "propose" or "suggest": the translation "strikes across" brings in the original physical sense which Rilke was always trying to uncover in any word.

Lines 70–71:   . . . *Angel,*
                to you I'll point it out. . . .

34. *B. 1907–1914*, 121 (dated January 18, 1911).
35. *Briefe an einen jungen Dichter* (Leipzig, 1929), 45.
36. *B. aus M.*, 335 (dated November 13, 1925).

the angel of the Elegies is that creature in whom the transformation of the visible into the invisible which we are accomplishing, can already be seen completed. For the angel of the Elegies, towers and palaces long since gone, still exist, *because* long since invisible; and the towers and bridges of our life that are still standing are *already* invisible for the angel, though they remain quite physical for us. The angel of the Elegies is that being who vouches for the recognition of a higher order of reality in the invisible—therefore is "terrible" to us because we still hang on to the visible even though we are its lovers and transformers.[37]

Line 82: . . . *Chartres was great* . . .

Chartres struck me as being much more ravaged than Notre Dame de Paris. Much more hopeless; much more prey to those who destroy. From the first impression, the way it rises up, like a great cloak, and then the first detail, that slender weather-beaten angel holding out a sundial exposed to the day's full circle of hours. . . . We got to the cathedral about nine-thirty; the sun had gone under, there was a gray frost; it was still very quiet . . . we stood like damned souls compared to the angel as he held out his dial ecstatically to the sun he always saw. . . .[38]

EIGHTH ELEGY

Line 1: . . . *all creatures* . . .

these confidants of the whole of existence, the animals, who are evident to themselves in a wider cross-section of awareness, can most readily guide us to the other side and are close to the medial state.[39]

Line 52: *O blessedness of tiny creatures,*

That a multitude of creatures that spring from seeds exposed out-of-doors have *that*, that wide, sensitive, candid way of relating

37. *Ibid.*, 337.
38. *B. 1902–1906*, 294–295 (dated January 26, 1906).
39. *B. aus M.*, 283–284 (dated August 11, 1924).

to the womb—how much at home they must feel, in that respect, their whole lives long—in fact they do nothing but leap for joy in their mother's womb like little John the Baptist. For the same space received and delivered them and they never left its security.[40]

The Eighth Elegy is dedicated to Rudolf Kassner, the Austrian writer. He and Rilke had become friends at Duino where he had also been a frequent guest. The dedication, as Kassner suggested in an essay written in 1935,[41] may have been connected with a conversation they had had at Duino: Rilke had spoken then too about the "inner happiness of the gnat."

Line 58: . . . *like the soul of an Etruscan*

In Etruscan tombs the souls of the dead were represented as birds painted on the tomb walls.

NINTH ELEGY

Lines 2–4: *like the laurel* . . .
           the margin of each leaf fluted
           with small waves (like a wind's smile) . . .

Laurel leaves have a straight central vein running between the two wavy outer edges—similar to the lines made by two lips closed in a smile.

Line 26: . . . *under the stars* . . . they *are* better *left untold.*

Rilke is referring not to the stars in our sky, but rather to those that configure the mythical tales of his special constellations.

40. *RMR-LAS*, 396 (dated February 20, 1918).
41. *Buch der Erinnerung*, 317.

TENTH ELEGY

Line 62: . . . *land of lamentation*

Rilke wrote to Witold von Hulewicz that the Elegies tried to establish the transformation of the visible into the invisible as a kind of "norm of existence":

they assert and celebrate this consciousness. They relate it cautiously to its origins, claiming ancient traditions and rumors of traditions to support the theory, and even invoke a foreknowledge of such relationships in the Egyptian cult of the dead. (Although the "Land of Lamentation" through which the older Lament leads the dead youth is *not to be identified* with Egypt, but is only, so to speak, a reflection of the Nile country in the desert clarity of the consciousness of the dead.)[42]

Line 82: . . . *rim of the crown.* . . .

The double crown of Upper and Lower Egypt worn by the Sphinx and by all rulers after the unification of the two halves of the country.

Lines 85–86: *faintly inscribes on the new hearing*
of the dead, . . .

In his 1919 essay, *Das Ur-Geräusch* (*Primal Sound*), Rilke tells how the lines in a skull suture once reminded him of those cut on the wax cylinder of an early phonograph. If a phonograph needle were to play on the grooves of a skull, he asks,

what would happen? A sound would be produced, a sequence of sounds, a kind of music. . . . What contour could not be completed so to speak, in this way, so that it may break out, make itself felt in another field of sense?[43]

42. *B. aus M.*, 336–337 (dated November 13, 1925).
43. *G.W.*, iv, 290.

Rilke felt that this extended awareness might be experienced in many places:

The grain of wood, the movement of an insect: our eye is trained to follow these things and obscure them. What a godsend to our hearing if we could transform these zigzags into auditory events.[44]

In the Tenth Elegy this new sensory experience of *hearing*, for example, the contours of the face of the Sphynx when an owl's wing brushed across it, is an illustration of the extended awareness of the dead.

Lines 90–92: . . . *the* Rider, *the* Staff, . . .
　　　　　 . . . *Fruit-garland* . . .
　　　　　 Cradle; Way; *the* Burning Book; Doll;
　　　　　 Window.

These imaginary constellations are all representations of pain or heaviness: the weight of the rider on a horse, ripe fruit falling, the doll, etc.

Lines 107–108: . . . *catkins hung
from the empty hazels,* . . .

Rilke had originally put "willows," but changed this to "hazels" on the advice of a friend who had done some research for him. He wrote to her some time in December 1921, when he was apparently working on the Elegy:

what a kind idea to introduce me so clearly and conclusively to the elements of "catkinology" with your parcel and accompanying letter. After this there is no need of any further or more detailed information: I am convinced! So, (oddly enough) there are no "hanging" willow catkins, and even if there were some rare, tropical exception, I wouldn't be able to use it anyway. The place in the poem, whose factual accuracy I wanted to verify, stands or falls on whether the reader can grasp and understand, with his

44. *B. aus M.*, 384 (dated April 5, 1926).

first intuition, simply this *falling* of the catkin; if he can't the image loses all meaning. So the absolutely *typical* appearance of this flowering has to be called up. . . . The shrub which years ago supplied the impression I've used in my work must have been a hazelnut whose branches where they are most closely packed develop long catkins that hang vertically, *before* the leaves come out. So I know what I needed to know and have changed "willow" to "hazel" in the text.[45]

ELEGY ON CHILDHOOD

Line 10: *childhood bears fruit.* . . .

The German word is *fruchtet* which also means "avails" or "is useful."

Lines 44–45: *. . . a doubting branch growing hard on the Judas-tree of choice.*

The German word for "growing hard" is *verholzen,* which in slang also means "to be spanked."

Line 47: *. . . gives it strange chill . . .*

Fear makes even a doll give one a chill.

45. *B. aus M.,* 71–72.

BIBLIOGRAPHY

RILKE: WORKS AND LETTERS
(ABBREVIATIONS USED IN FOOTNOTES ARE
INDICATED BY BRACKETS)

Gesammelte Werke, Bd. 1-6 (Leipzig: Insel-Verlag, 1930)
[*G.W.*]

Sämtliche Werke, Bd. 1-6 (Wiesbaden: Insel-Verlag, 1966)
[*S.W.*]

Briefe aus den Jahren 1902-1906 (Leipzig: Insel-Verlag,
1929) [*B. 1902-1906*]

Briefe aus den Jahren 1906-1907 (Leipzig: Insel-Verlag,
1930) [*B. 1906-1907*]

Briefe aus den Jahren 1907-1914 (Leipzig: Insel-Verlag,
1933) [*B. 1907-1914*]

Briefe aus den Jahren 1914-1921 (Leipzig: Insel-Verlag,
1937) {*B. 1914-1921*]

Briefe aus Muzot 1921-1926 (Leipzig: Insel-Verlag, 1935)
[*B. aus M.*]

*Rainer Maria Rilke–Marie von Thurn und Taxis: Brief-
wechsel*, Bd. 1-2 (Zurich: Niehaus & Rokitansky Verlag,
1951) [*RMR-MTT*]

Rainer Maria Rilke–Lou Andreas-Salomé: Briefwechsel (Zurich: Max Niehans Verlag, 1952).
Briefe an seinen Verleger, Bd. 1–2 (Wiesbaden: Insel-Verlag, 1949) [*B. Verleger*]
Briefe an eine junge Frau (Leipzig: Insel-Verlag, 1930)
Briefe an einen jungen Dichter (Leipzig: Insel-Verlag, 1929)

CRITICAL WORKS

Bassermann, Dieter, *Der Späte Rilke* (Munich: Leibniz-Verlag, 1947)

Batterby, K. A. J., *Rilke and France* (Oxford, University Press, 1966)

Butler, E. M., *Rainer Maria Rilke* (Cambridge, University Press, 1966)

Guardini, Romano, *Rilke's Duino Elegies* (Chicago: Regnery, 1961)

Hartman, Geoffrey H., *The Unmediated Vision* (New Haven: Yale University Press, 1954)

Heller, Erich, *The Artist's Journey into the Interior* (New York: Random House, 1968)

———, *The Disinherited Mind* (New York: World, 1961)

Hattingberg, Magda von, *Rilke und Benvenuta* (Vienna: Andermann, 1943)

Heerikhuizen, F. W. van, *Rainer Maria Rilke, His Life and Work* (London: Routledge, 1951)

Kassner, Rudolf, *Buch der Erinnerung* (Leipzig: Insel-Verlag, 1938)

Mason, E. C., *Lebenshaltung und Symbolik bei Rainer Maria Rilke* (Weimar: H. Bohlaus Verlag, 1939)

———, *Rilke, Europe and the English-Speaking World* (Cambridge, Univ. Press, 1961)

Purtscher-Wydenbruch, Nora, *Rilke, Man and Poet* (London: Lehmann, 1949)

Ritzer, Walter, *Rainer Maria Rilke Bibliographie* (Vienna: O. Kerry Verlag, 1951)

Salis, J. R. von, *Rainer Maria Rilke, The Years in Switzerland*, trans. N. K. Cruickshank (London: Hogarth, 1964)

Thurn und Taxis-Hohenlohe, Fürstin Marie von, *Erinnerungen an Rainer Maria Rilke* (Munich: R. Oldenbourg, 1932)

BIBLIOGRAPHY

Rilke, Wilhelm. *Rainer Maria Rilke* ... Leipzig: Insel-Verlag, ...

... *Die Briefe an einen jungen Dichter* ...

... *Prose and Verse*, ed. ... Cambridge: London, ...

... *und Text. Herausgegeben* ... Müller ...

... *Rainer Maria Rilke*, Munich: R. Oldenbourg ...